The Beginner's Guide to
FRIENDSHIP
BRACELETS

Essential Lessons for Creating Stylish Designs to Wear and Give

Maria Makarova, aka

Masha Knots

The Beginner's Guide to Friendship Bracelets
Maria Makarova, aka Masha Knots

Editor: Kelly Reed
Project manager: Lisa Brazieal
Marketing coordinator: Katie Walker
Copyeditor: Joan Dixon
Page Composition: Kim Scott/Bumpy Design
Interior Design: Aren Straiger
Cover production: Aren Straiger
Cover photographs: Maria Makarova

ISBN: 978-1-68198-861-0

1st Edition (2nd printing, October 2024)
© 2022 Maria Makarova
All photographs © Maria Makarova

Rocky Nook Inc.
1010 B Street, Suite 350
San Rafael, CA 94901
USA

www.rockynook.com

Distributed in the UK and Europe by Publishers Group UK

Distributed in the U.S. and all other territories by Publishers Group West

Library of Congress Control Number: 2021944848

TABLE OF CONTENTS

Introduction

Hello, hello! My name is Maria, but most people know me as Masha Knots. You may know me from my tutorials and entertainment videos about friendship bracelets on my YouTube channel. I've been making friendship bracelets since 2009 after a friend showed me how to make the candy stripe and chevron patterns, and I immediately fell in love with the craft. I soon learned there were bracelet patterns that allowed me to create nearly any design I could imagine and that blew my mind. And as they say, the rest is history!

In this book I aim to share some of my friendship bracelet knowledge in a fun and understandable way. I will tell you about what friendship bracelets are as well as the various types that exist and the techniques used to make them. I will show you the types of strings I like to use as well as other materials that will help you create or customize your bracelets. I will teach you all about basic knots, various starts and ends to your bracelets, and other knotting techniques. I will show you examples of simple bracelets, which you can jump straight into creating. I will also explain normal and alpha patterns and the differences between them, and I will teach you how to properly read patterns.

I will go over some common beginner mistakes and how to fix them, and I will share a wide range of tips and tricks I have picked up over the years. I will also cover the various types of embellishments you can add when you want your bracelets to have a little extra pizazz. At the end of this book you will find a photo gallery showing some of my favorite bracelets I have created. I hope this will give you some inspiration for designs you want to try!

Thank you for picking up my book. I hope you enjoy it and I want to give you a warm welcome to the world of friendship bracelets.

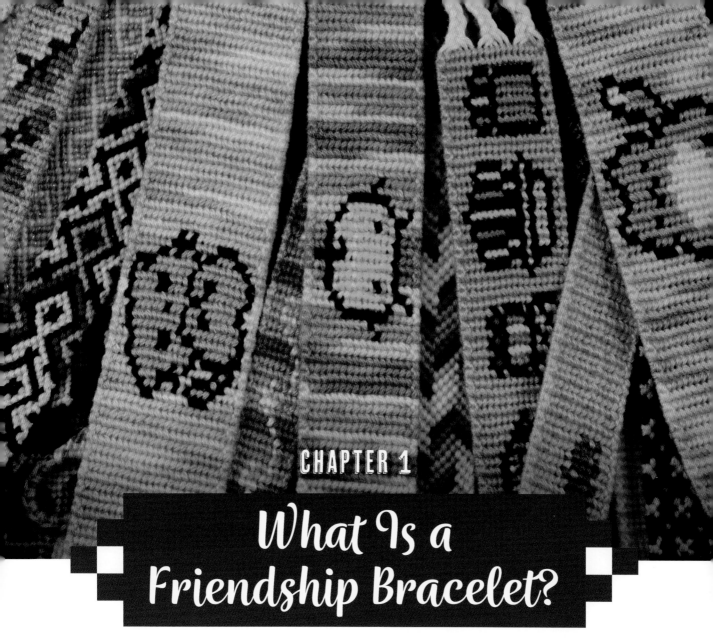

CHAPTER 1

What Is a Friendship Bracelet?

Friendship bracelets have been around for thousands of years, and the art of making them spans multiple generations and cultures. People create and wear friendship bracelets for a wide variety of reasons. As the name suggests, many people make and gift these bracelets as an expression of friendship. Knotting a bracelet for a friend or loved one is a beautiful way of expressing how much you care for them, and wearing a bracelet made by a friend will always remind you of them.

However, many people also wear bracelets simply as a beautiful accessory or because creating friendship bracelets is a fun hobby. Self-expression and creativity are also common reasons for people to create friendship bracelets.

TYPES OF BRACELETS

There are three main types of friendship bracelets: normal bracelets, alpha bracelets, and special bracelets.

Normal patterns are knotted diagonally and all the strings work in combination with the others—all the strings are used to make knots onto the other strings—to create the design. Normal patterns can be used to create beautiful, intricate designs.

Alpha bracelets are knotted horizontally and are created by making knots with leading strings onto base strings, which are not visible within the completed bracelet. Alpha patterns can be used to create detailed, picture-like designs as well as designs that have text within them.

Special bracelets encompass a wide category of bracelets that include virtually all the other types of bracelets that don't fit into the category of normal or alpha. Special bracelets can be created using a variety of techniques, sometimes using elements from normal or alpha bracelets, or even from both or neither. The majority of these bracelets require following a video tutorial to create since they often include modifications that cannot be easily represented within a bracelet pattern alone.

There are, of course, other types of bracelets made with thread that look similar to the standard friendship bracelets. Kumihimo bracelets, macramé bracelets, and even braided bracelets are all examples of other techniques that can be used to create beautiful designs out of strings.

In this book you will find explanations and instructions for creating normal bracelets, alpha bracelets, and some special bracelets, as well as fun inspiration for creating your own bracelet designs.

LEARNING MORE: VIDEO TUTORIALS

Video tutorials can be helpful for beginner and advanced bracelet makers. On my YouTube channel (youtube.com/MashaKnots) you will find beginner-friendly tutorials as well as tutorials for more advanced knotters on specific bracelet patterns, techniques, strings and materials, types of starts and ends, and much more!

My *Knot with Me* playlist on YouTube contains time-lapse videos where I demonstrate knotting various bracelets, which can help you see the decisions I make when segment knotting normal patterns, or the way I switch my colors and make sure my rows are still straight when knotting alpha patterns.

New tutorials, time lapses, bracelet discussions, and just fun bracelet-related videos are constantly being uploaded. I would love to connect with you there too!

OTHER ONLINE COMMUNITIES AND PATTERNS

The website BraceletBook.com acts as a social network for friendship bracelet makers and has thousands of active users who post new patterns, photos, photo and video tutorials, and forum discussions daily. Joining this online community would be beneficial to beginner bracelet makers as members are always happy to help answer questions and give tips and pointers about the craft.

Another great way to find fellow bracelet makers is via Instagram. My personal Instagram (@masha_knots) contains photos of my bracelets, time-lapse videos of bracelet creation, and even short video tutorials for specific patterns or techniques.

Searching through hashtags such as #friendshipbracelets and #fenechki, which is the Russian word for friendship bracelets and contains thousands of posts from the very active Russian knotting community, can help you connect with fellow knotters and inspire you to create even more beautiful bracelets.

Discord is another great place where you will find a community of bracelet makers. I have my own Discord server on which you can connect with fellow knotters about anything bracelet related—ask questions, show off your bracelets, or share your favorite patterns. For times when you want to talk to like-minded people about things other than bracelet making, there are also channels for other topics on Discord such as a pet photos channel, a fandom chat, and even a study chat.

Of course, other online spaces for bracelet makers exist but since not everything can be mentioned here, I will leave finding more of them up to you!

CHAPTER 2

String Types

I want to start this chapter off by saying that you don't have to use the same materials as me, or anyone else, to create beautiful bracelets. Looking at other people's creations, while often inspiring, can sometimes be discouraging if you compare your work to theirs. It may seem like the one thing you're missing in order to create bracelets just like theirs is the specific material they used. This is not true! Comparing yourself to others rarely does you any good because the reality is that people learn at different rates, and they create and knot in different ways. If you give 10 knotters identical materials and patterns, you will have 10 unique bracelets as a result. The materials, or even the specific brands someone uses, has little to do with the result they achieve, and you absolutely can make beautiful bracelets with a limited string collection. This chapter is intended as an overview of what materials are out there to help you get an idea of how you could potentially expand your collection down the line when you are ready for more variety and creativity. Try not to get overwhelmed and start by using the strings and other materials that are readily available to you.

There are many types of string you can use. Most people use embroidery floss, which is what I will be using throughout this book and what I would recommend a beginner to use, but you can also use special craft thread or even yarn. Let's go over the differences between these string types and take a look at some variations.

made of 100% cotton, and this is one of the reasons people prefer using it to other types of string.

EMBROIDERY FLOSS

Embroidery floss is the most used material for friendship bracelet making. It typically consists of six individual strands that are loosely twisted into a single thread, but unlike in embroidery or cross stitch, you rarely need to separate the individual strands in bracelet making. Embroidery floss is most commonly

CRAFT THREAD

Craft thread is a less common material, though it can be very useful for making friendship bracelets. Craft thread is similar to embroidery floss in width and in the fact that it also consists of several small strands of string braided together. However, the main difference is that craft thread does not separate and fray as easily as embroidery floss. This is one of the main reasons some people prefer using craft thread. Because it doesn't fray, it is a great material for beginners, plus it is commonly sold in large packs containing a variety of colors. The main downside to craft thread, however, is that it isn't as widely available and can be harder to find than regular embroidery floss. Another downside is that there tends to be a limited range of colors. While there are definitely enough colors for a beginner—in fact, I used my craft thread collection exclusively for more than five years—once you become more familiar with the craft you might desire a wider range of color options. Overall, craft thread is a great material to use, and I recommend it for beginners.

YARN AND CROCHET THREAD

Some yarns and crochet threads can also be used for friendship bracelet making. The main benefit of using these materials is the length at which they are typically sold. A typical skein of embroidery floss or craft thread is eight meters long whereas yarns or crochet threads can be hundreds of meters in length. However, the downside of these materials is simply the fact that they weren't created with friendship bracelet making in mind. They are designed for different purposes; most yarns are either too thick or too fluffy for friendship bracelets, and most crochet threads are too thin and some too slippery to work with comfortably. Due to the differences in elasticity and sizes, the knots produced by these materials will also vary in size. This can create problems when knotting bracelets as keeping your knots roughly the same size helps balance the bracelet and ensures that the pattern is correctly represented. There are, of course, both yarns and crochet threads that can work perfectly for friendship bracelets, but they can be quite hard to find. Also, the initial appearance of a type of yarn can be deceiving, and only through trial and error can you figure out which brand fits your needs.

Finding yarn or crochet thread that works for you can be extremely rewarding. The ability to use as much of it as you desire without having to worry about it quickly running out is freeing. Additionally, yarns and crochet threads tend to be the materials that have the most variety when it comes to special string, which we will discuss next.

SPECIAL STRINGS

Special strings can be loosely defined as strings that aren't made of a basic material or a solid color. The most common special string types are metallics, sparkly strings, and multicolored strings.

METALLIC STRINGS

Metallic strings are typically made from polyester and are very sparkly. Most commonly, this string is made as a variation of embroidery floss, though there are metallic yarns and crochet threads too. The main benefit is, of course, the beautiful sparkle and shine it adds to your bracelets. The downside, however, is the fact that it is rather difficult to work with. Due to the materials it is made from, metallic string tends to be very slippery, which makes knots it creates prone to unknotting no matter how hard you tie them. Additionally, again due to its slipperiness, the individual strands making up the metallic thread tend to separate rather easily, which makes working with it challenging as it acts more like six tiny strings rather than a single string. The knots that metallic strings produce are often larger than knots made from regular embroidery floss, which makes pairing it with other strings within a bracelet difficult as the bracelet becomes unbalanced with knots that differ in size.

TIPS & TRICKS

Tie a little knot at the ends of each of your metallic strings to keep them from separating.

If your knots are too big, try separating the strands of your thread. Typically, a string is made up of six strands, so try using three instead. This will make your knots smaller and might help blend them in with knots made by other strings.

SPARKLY STRINGS

Sparkly string is similar to metallic string as it also sparkles. However, metallic string is sparkly in its entirety whereas sparkly string tends to have a sparkly filament wound over string of a solid color. When used within a bracelet, unlike metallic string, which produces a bright sparkle in every knot, sparkly string is more varied and unpredictable, sprinkling in the sparkles every so often. Sparkly string is most commonly found as yarn or crochet thread, though there are some brands of embroidery floss that have

sparkly options. Depending on the type of string you buy, the knot sizes produced by it might differ, but there are plenty of strings out there that are perfect for bracelet making. The downside of using sparkly thread is that it cannot be 100% cotton due to the sparkly filament. Another downside is that the sparkly filament easily separates at the ends from the rest of the string. Despite the downsides, sparkly string is a personal favorite of mine and I love finding creative ways to use it within a bracelet.

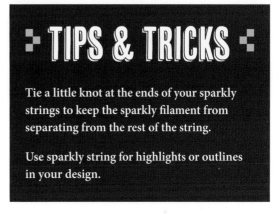

⁘ TIPS & TRICKS ⁘

Tie a little knot at the ends of your sparkly strings to keep the sparkly filament from separating from the rest of the string.

Use sparkly string for highlights or outlines in your design.

MULTICOLORED STRING

Multicolored string comes as embroidery floss, craft thread, yarn, crochet thread, or really any other kind of material you can think of to use in your friendship bracelets. Multicolored string is probably the most common type of special string you will find, and it is also arguably the most versatile. This string type has several subtypes based on color palettes. Monochrome multicolored strings fade from one shade of a color to another shade of that same color within the strand. Gradient multicolored strings blend several colors that are close to each other on the color wheel to create a beautiful gradient. Other color palettes also exist, seamlessly blending a vast variety of color combinations. My favorite is rainbow multicolored thread, though from personal experience this is the most difficult variety to find. Multicolored thread holds the characteristics of whatever material it is made of.

CHAPTER 3

Useful Bracelet-Making Tools

There are a wide range of tools and materials that can be useful in friendship bracelet creation. Some of these materials can even help you create things that aren't necessarily bracelets but that use the same knotting techniques and styles, like keychains or wall hangings. Other materials can make the knotting process easier or can enhance your creations. Let's discuss some of the more common materials used.

SECURING YOUR BRACELETS

Different knotters prefer different ways of securing their bracelets to their workspace. Tape, safety pins, and even clipboards or just clip-ons can all work to keep your bracelet in place while you are working on it. This is a matter of personal preference, and finding the method that's right for you requires a little experimentation.

TAPE

Your bracelet can be secured directly onto your workspace with tape. The main benefit of this method is its simplicity and convenience. Additionally, using tape is great for filming as it keeps your bracelet steady as you knot. However, there are also drawbacks to tape—the sticky residue being the main one. There are many varieties of tape that could work for you, but my personal preference is masking or painter's tape as it gets the job done without leaving any residue, and you can easily tear it off the roll. Another drawback to using tape is the fact that sometimes strings slip out from under it. Using a few pieces of tape along the length of your strings (which

you can later use to create the ties of the bracelet) helps increase adhesion and decreases the chance of a string slipping out.

If your bracelet has a loop, take a piece of scrap thread, place it between the loop, and tape that thread down to secure your bracelet.

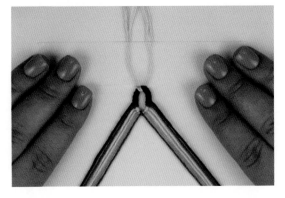

SAFETY PINS

Safety pins can be used to pin a bracelet down to a surface such as a cushion or your jeans. The beauty of this method is that it's mobile. You aren't tied down to a specific place and you can even knot in public places or while on public transport. The drawback to using safety pins is simple—it can be painful to accidentally stab yourself with the pin, so take extra care when using them.

A great way to use a safety pin for securing a bracelet is by making three incisions with the pin: one before the bracelet, one through the bracelet or in the middle of its loop, and one after. This method secures your bracelet in place without creating unnecessary holes within it.

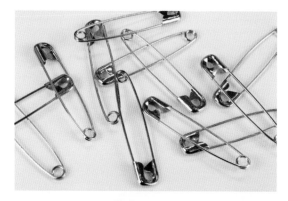

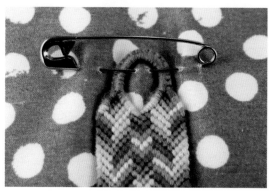

KEYRINGS AND DOWELS

Friendship bracelet-making skills can be used for more than just bracelets! The same knotting techniques can be used to create unique keychains and wall hangings.

Various types of keychains and keyrings can be used. My personal favorites are simple rings or the D-shaped swivel clasps used for keychains.

As with keychains, various types of dowels can be used to create wall hangings. My personal favorites are wooden dowels that are 15cm long and 4mm in diameter. I find this size is the most versatile for the type of wall hangings I make.

To attach strings to a keyring or a dowel you need to make a lark's head knot, which will be explained in chapter 4.

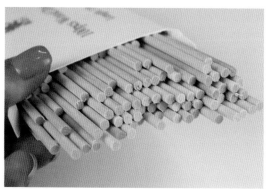

STORING YOUR STRINGS AND BRACELETS

Each crafter has their own unique system of storing their strings, materials, and bracelets. Whether you use boxes, bags, or displays, finding a system that works for you will be individual to your circumstances and preferences.

During my time as a bracelet maker, I have gone through several storage systems for both my strings and my bracelets. I started off with an old shoebox that I filled with a knotted mess of all the string I owned. My bracelets were shoved in that same box. As you can imagine, this was not the best storage system. I moved on to using separate shoeboxes based on string type, or rather strings I preferred and strings I liked less, and my bracelet collection moved to a small jewelry box.

A couple of years ago I decided enough was enough and I organized my strings into plastic embroidery floss storage boxes that I bought online. I used an embroidery floss bobbin winder and spent weeks winding individual skeins of string onto plastic bobbins. I then carefully placed them into the storage boxes in an aesthetic fashion. The result was

beautiful! I ended up with a stack of several boxes filled with string. The bobbins kept my string from tangling, making it incredibly easy to just measure and cut. You can watch the video of my winding and organization process on my YouTube channel by searching for the video titled *Organizing My Thread Collection.*

I quickly found that I kept forgetting to put the strings back into the box when I was done using them, and I never seemed to use strings from the boxes that were at the top of the stack. Moreover, winding the string took me so much time and effort that I never wanted to repeat that process, despite how satisfying it was. I soon realized this system was not ideal for me.

Of course, your storage system depends entirely on personal preference. There are plenty of crafters who love their bobbin boxes and swear by them, but I have since moved on to a different storage system. These days I store strings by type and color. My main supply of string consists of solid color embroidery floss. I sorted the strings and bobbins into groups by color: reds go together, greens go together, and so on. I placed these color groups into individual zip lock bags, which are stored in a box with a lid. I still use bobbins to keep my strings from becoming a tangled mess, but I only load the bobbins when I start using a new string. If a string is still in its original wrapper, completely untouched, it is unlikely to tangle with other strings.

My special yarns, sparkly strings, and multicolored strings—as well as my blacks and whites—are stored separately. Blacks and whites live in a small box near the colored embroidery floss but are kept separate as I use them frequently. My special strings and yarns, which I use less often, are stored in one of my table drawers. I now store my completed bracelets stacked inside a box, as you can see in the image below. Feel free to utilize whatever storage method works best for you!

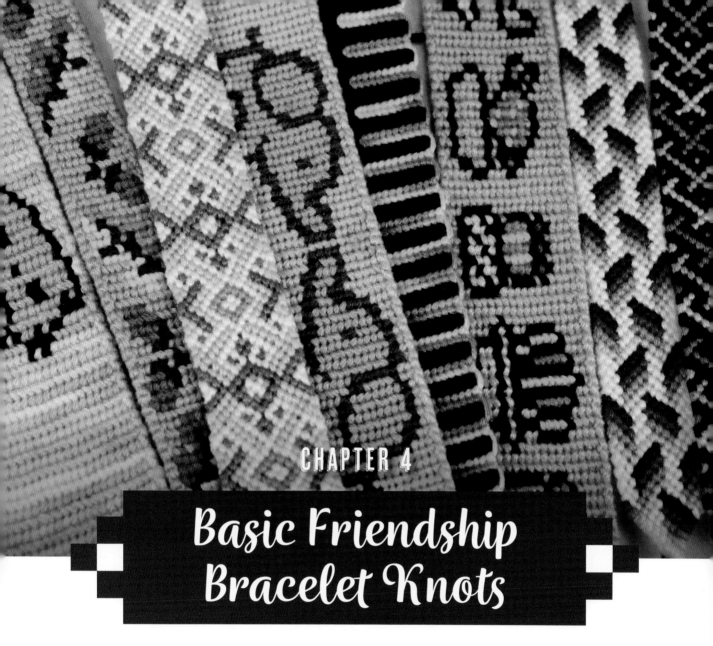

CHAPTER 4

Basic Friendship Bracelet Knots

In this chapter we will look at the four main knots used in friendship bracelet making as well as the lark's head knot, which is sometimes used to attach strings to a keychain or dowel, and the overhand knot, which is often used to create a beginner's loop or to tie off your strings at the end of your bracelet.

There are four basic knots used in friendship bracelet making that you will likely find in every pattern you decide to make. Each of these knots has a different function within the bracelet and is represented by a specific type of arrow in a pattern. These bracelet knots each consist of two half knots. The way each half knot is made is what differentiates each full knot from one another.

Typically, knots are made between two individual strings but in some cases, they can be made between one string and a group of multiple strings or between two groups of multiple strings. However, knots using multiple strings can't be well represented in a pattern. If a bracelet or a technique requires knots between multiple strings, it would be what we call a "special bracelet" or a "bracelet technique" and would usually require a separate tutorial. If you are making bracelets based on patterns alone, it is more than likely that the represented knots are to be made between two individual strings.

The four basic knots are as follows:

- The Forward knot
- The Backward knot
- The Forward-Backward knot
- The Backward-Forward knot

Let's take a closer look at these four basic knots.

The Forward Knot

The function of a forward knot is to switch the positions of the two strings while making a knot of the *left* string's color.

In a pattern, the forward knot is typically represented by a circle with an arrow pointing to the *right*. The color of the circle represents the color of the knot created and will always be the color of the *left* string going into the knot.

When creating a knot, I like to use one hand to hold the string I'm making the knot onto and use the other hand to hold the string I'm making the knot with. In a forward knot, since we are moving the left string to the right, I like to use my right hand to make the knot. Not everyone changes hands depending on the direction of the knot they are making, but since this is how I do it, this is how I will demonstrate the process.

Following are the steps used to create a forward knot:

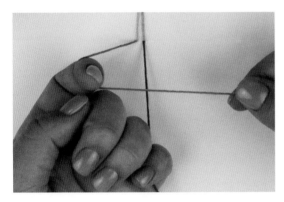

1. Take the string you will be making a knot onto. At the start it will be the one on the right. Grip it with the pinky finger on your left hand. Pull the string toward you slightly so it is a little tight, making it easier to work with.

With your right hand, take the string you will be making the knot with. At the start it will be the string on the left. Stick out your left index finger and loop the string over it with your right hand. Drag the left string across the right string so the left string is on top. The result should look like you're making the shape of the number 4 with your strings.

2. Now extend your right index finger and put it into the loop of the "4" shape that you created and push it under the string you're making your knot onto.

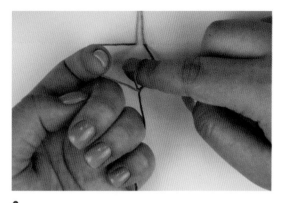 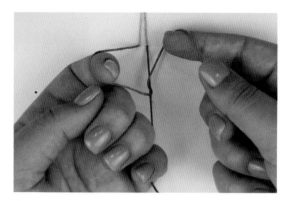

3. Still using your right index finger, use your nail to catch the string you're making the knot with.

4. Use your right index finger to twist the string you're making the knot with and pull it through and out of the loop.

Before we continue, let's pause and have a look at what the knot looks like at this point. All we've done is twist the string we're making the knot with (the left string originally) onto the other string (the right string originally).

 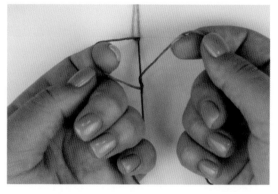

5. Pull the string you're making the knot with up until it sits where you would like the finished knot to be. At this point we have created the first half of the forward knot.

6. To create the second half of the knot, we must repeat steps 1–5. The second half should look something like the image above.

7. To complete the knot, pull the string up once more. The forward knot is now complete! Notice how the strings have switched positions and the knot is the color of the string that was originally on the left.

The Backward Knot

The function of a backward knot is to switch the positions of the two strings while making a knot of the *right* string's color.

In a pattern, a backward knot is typically represented by a circle with an arrow pointing to the *left*. The color of the circle represents the color of the knot created and will always be the color of the string on the *right* that creates the knot.

A backward knot is a mirror image of a forward knot. I like to switch the hand I make the knot with when making a backward knot. Since the right string is moving from right to left, I like to use my left hand to make the knot.

Below are the steps used to make a backward knot:

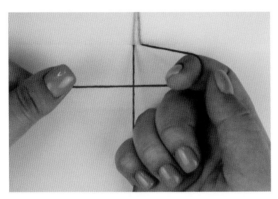

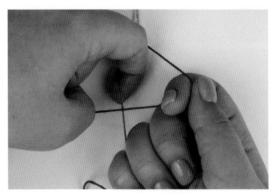

1. Take the string on the left—the string you will be making the knot onto—and grip it with the pinky finger on your right hand. Pull the string toward you slightly so it is a little tight, making it easier to work with.

With your left hand, take the string you will be making the knot with. At the start it will be the string on the right. Stick out your right index finger and loop the string over it with your left hand. Drag the right string across the left string so the right string is on top. The result should look like a mirror image of the shape of the number 4 with your strings.

2. Now extend your left index finger and put it into the loop of the mirrored "4" shape that you have created and push it under the string you're making your knot onto.

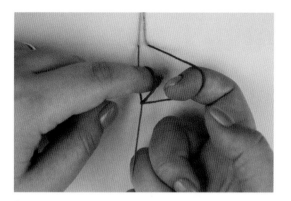

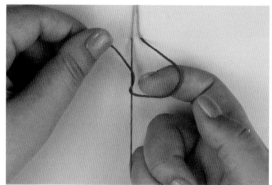

3. Still using your left index finger, with your nail catch the string you're making the knot.

4. Use your left index finger to twist the string you're making the knot with and pull it through and out of the loop.

Before we continue, let's pause and have a look at what the knot looks like at this point. As with the forward knot, all we've done is twist the string we're making the knot with (the right string originally) onto the other string (the left string originally).

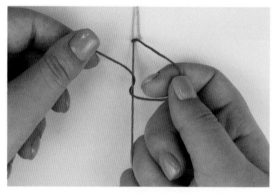

5. Pull the string you're making the knot with up until it sits where you would like the finished knot to be. At this point we have created the first *half* of the backward knot.

6. To complete the knot, we must repeat steps 1–5. The second half of the knot should look something like this example.

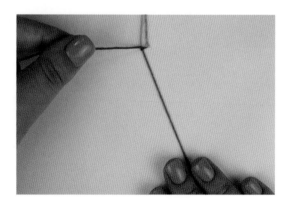

7. To complete the knot, pull the string up once more. The backward knot is now complete! Notice how the strings have switched positions but, opposite to the forward knot, the knot itself is the color of the string that was originally on the right.

The Forward-Backward Knot

The function of a forward-backward knot is to make a knot of the *left* string's color without switching the two strings' original positions.

In a pattern, a forward-backward knot is typically represented by a circle with an arrow pointing to the *right and back*. The color of the circle represents the color of the knot created and will always be the color of the *left* string going into the knot.

The forward-backward knot, just like the forward knot and the backward knot, consists of two half knots. Unlike the forward knot and the backward knot, these two half knots are not the same. In fact, to create the forward-backward knot you must do one half of a forward knot followed by one half of a backward knot with the same string. I will demonstrate this for you.

1. First, follow steps 1–5 of the forward knot. This first half knot will look identical to the first half of a regular forward knot.

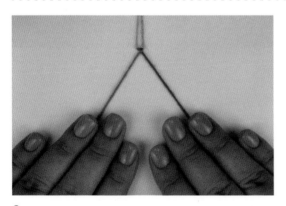
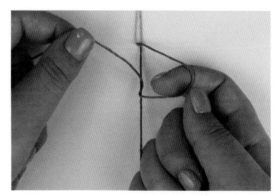

2. Continue by making half of a backward knot as described in steps 1–5 of the backward knot. Use the same string to make the knot with as you did for the half forward knot. I like to switch hands at this point so that is how I will be demonstrating. Once you've created the second half knot your knot should look like this picture.

The forward-backward knot is now complete! Unlike the forward knot or backward knot, the strings have stayed in their original positions, but the knot created is the color of the string on the left.

The Backward-Forward Knot

The function of a backward-forward knot is to make a knot of the *right* string's color without switching the two strings' positions.

In a pattern, a backward-forward knot is typically represented by a circle with an arrow pointing to the *left and back*. The color of the circle represents the color of the knot created and will always be the color of the *right* string going into the knot.

The backward-forward knot, like all the other knots we have discussed, consists of two half knots. Like the forward-backward knot, the two half knots are not the same. To create a backward-forward knot you must do one half of a backward knot followed by one half of a forward knot with the same string. Here, I will demonstrate how to make a backward-forward knot:

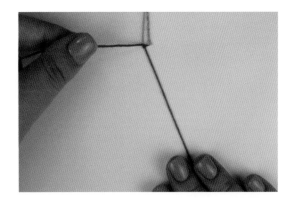

1. First, follow steps 1–5 of a backward knot. The first half knot will look identical to the first half of a regular backward knot.

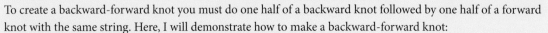

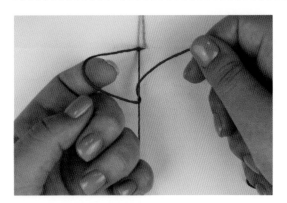
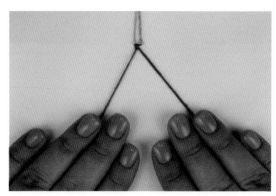

2. Continue by making half of a forward knot as described in steps 1–5 of a forward knot. Use the same string to make the knot with as you did for the first half backward knot. I like to switch hands at this point, so this is how I will be demonstrating. Once you've created the second half knot, your knot should look like this example.

The backward-forward knot is now complete! Just like with the forward-backward knot, the strings stayed in their original positions, but the knot created is the color of the string on the right.

The Lark's Head Knot

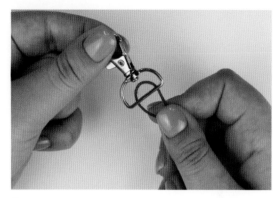

1. The lark's head knot is commonly used to attach strings to something like a keyring or a dowel. To create a lark's head knot, simply fold your string and place it under whatever you want to attach it to.

2. Grab the loop of the string and fold it over what you are attaching it to.

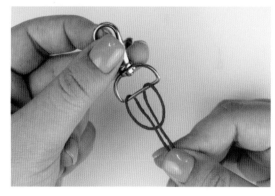

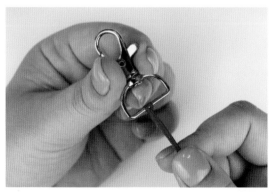

3. Pull the ends of your strings through the loop. Your lark's head knot is now complete.

The Overhand Knot

The overhand knot is often used to create beginner's loops and to tie off strings at the end of your bracelet.

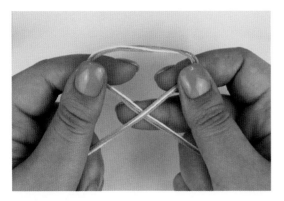

1. Fold one group of ends of your strings over the other to create a loop.

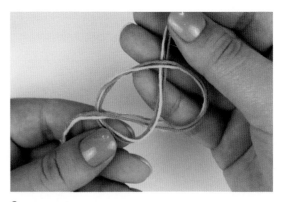

2. Grab the ends that are on the bottom and put them through and under the loop.

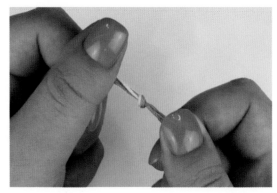

3. Pull on both groups of ends to tighten the knot. Your overhand knot is now complete.

TIPS & TRICKS

There are a few tips and tricks for making friendship bracelet knots that I've picked up over the years. I'd like to share these with you!

- When you are making a knot between two strings of the same color, it doesn't matter which type of knot you make. Whichever knot you choose, the color of the knot will always be the same since both strings are the same color. Choose the knot you feel most comfortable making and don't worry about what the pattern says.

- The first half knot you make is the one that determines the placement of your knot. The spot at which you stop pulling your string up when making the first half knot is where the completed knot will sit. When making a pattern, your aim is to position each knot between the two knots adjacent to it from the previous row.

- The second half knot you make is what secures your knot in place. If you forget to make the second half knot, your first one is likely to untangle and create a mess. Don't forget your second half knots!

- When pulling my strings up, I like to get quite close to the base of the string as I'm pulling it up. This allows for greater precision and control of the string and helps me get it to the exact place I want it to be.

- Practice, practice, practice! Practice really does make perfect and the more knots you make, the more you will get used to it and will start developing muscle memory. This helps your knots be consistent and thus helps your bracelets look cohesive. Remember to practice all the knot types so you don't get used to making one type more than the others. You will find videos demonstrating each knot on my YouTube channel if you'd like to see them in action.

CHAPTER 5

Simple Bracelets

Before you start learning about reading bracelet patterns, it is a good idea to make a few simple brace-lets to practice the basic friendship bracelet knots. In this chapter I will explain how to make a few of my favorite beginner-friendly bracelets. The bracelets in this chapter are organized in order of difficulty, from easiest to hardest. I recommend you start with the Classic Chevron bracelet before trying any other bracelets in this chapter.

Classic Chevron Bracelet

The Classic Chevron bracelet is a perfect bracelet for beginners to make as it uses both the forward and backward knots equally, making sure you get an equal amount of practice for both. The Chevron bracelet pattern is what we call a *normal* pattern. You can tell this by the fact that the knotting structure is diagonal.

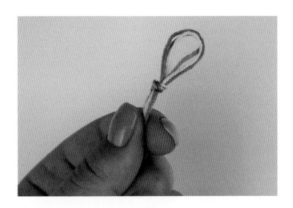

1. Start by picking your colors. You can choose as many colors as you like. The more colors you choose, the wider your bracelet will be, the longer the strings will need to be, and the longer it will take to finish. I will choose three colors for this tutorial. For simplicity, cut one string per color, 6 feet in length. Fold the strings in half and make a beginner's loop, explained in chapter 9.

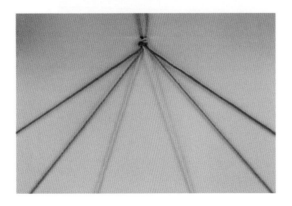

2. Start by arranging your strings. Separate them into two bundles with one string per color in each and lay them out symmetrically in the order that you want them to appear in your bracelet. Blue, pink, and yellow for me.

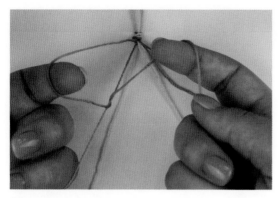

3. Grab the outermost string on the left side and make a forward knot onto the next string, which is just to the right of it.

4. Grab the next string and do another forward knot onto it with the same string. If you have more strings, continue making forward knots onto them in order until your string reaches the middle.

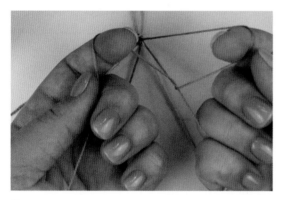

5. Next, grab the outermost string on the right side and do a backward knot onto the string that is just to the left of it.

6. Grab the next string and do another backward knot onto it with the same string. If you have more strings, continue making forward knots onto them in order until your string reaches the middle.

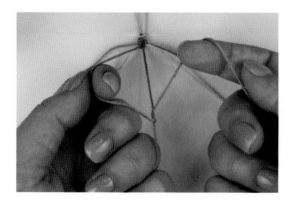

7. Once both of the strings are in the middle, make a knot between them. This can be any kind of knot as knots made with two strings of the same color will always be the same. Here I'll just make a forward knot.

The first row after a beginner's loop may look a bit wonky as the strings are just spreading out after a knot, but as long as you pay attention to the string order and the knots that you are making, it will even out as you go along.

Vertical Wave

The Vertical Wave bracelet is a personal favorite of mine as it is super simple to make but creates a fun and unique-looking bracelet. The vertical wave bracelet pattern is what we call an *alpha* pattern. You can tell this by the fact that the knotting structure is horizontal.

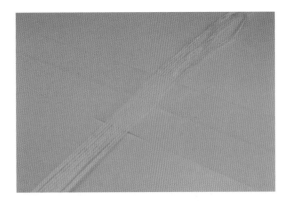

1. Start by determining the width of your bracelet by choosing several base strings. The more base strings, the wider your bracelet will be, the more strings you will need, and the longer it will take to complete. For this tutorial I will make my bracelet 10 strings wide. For simplicity, cut your base strings to be 1 yard in length. These base strings do not need to be the same color as the strings within your bracelet since these will be visible only in the ties of your bracelet. Secure the strings to your workspace, leaving enough extra string at the top to create your ties once you finish your bracelet.

2. Choose the two colors you want to alternate within your bracelet. Cut one string per color to be about 5 feet in length. You will likely have to replace your strings during the knotting process. Place these strings on your workspace—one to the left of your base strings and the other to the right of your base strings. These will be your leading strings.

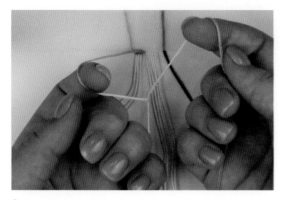

3. Grab the left leading string and make a row of forward knots along each of the base strings.

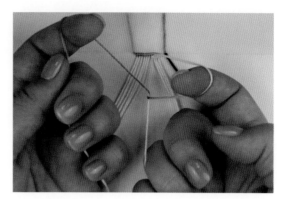

4. Once you reach the end, bring that leading string back by making a row of backward knots onto those same base strings.

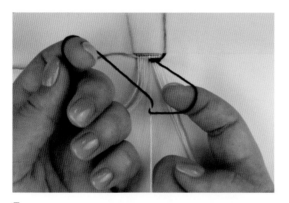

5. Next, grab your right leading string and make a row of backward knots along each of the base strings.

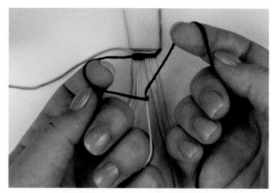

6. Once you reach the end, bring that leading string back by making a row of forward knots onto those same base strings.

REPLACING STRINGS

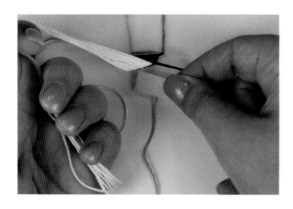

1. If at any point you run out of your leading string, cut a new string about 5 feet in length of that same color and secure it to your workspace behind your bracelet.

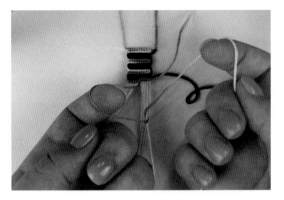

2. Next, make half of a row with your current leading string, bringing it to the middle of your bracelet. To switch the strings, make half of a knot with your new string.

3. Place the old string over it, pointing in the direction of your row, which is to the right in my case as my row is making forward knots.

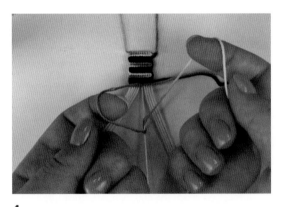

4. Use the new string to make to make the second half of your knot, ignoring the old string.

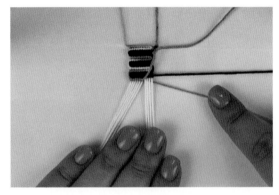

5. Tuck your old string into the back of your bracelet so it is out of the way. Once you make a few more rows, you can cut the old string off from the back of your bracelet as close as you can. It will not come undone.

Continue repeating these steps until the bracelet reaches the length you want. Once you're done, you can create ties for your bracelet. These are explained in chapter 9.

Chinese Staircase

The Chinese Staircase is a fun bracelet for beginners to make as it uses only one type of knot, is simple to make, and still produces a beautiful bracelet. Since this bracelet doesn't follow a pattern or the regular knotting structures, it falls into the category of what we call *special* bracelets.

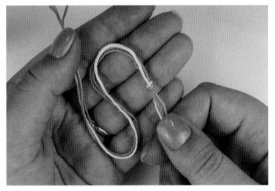

1. Start by choosing your colors. The more colors you choose, the thicker your bracelet will be and the longer the strings will need to be. For this tutorial I will choose three colors. For simplicity, cut one string per color, 1 yard in length. Make an overhand knot, leaving enough length at the end to make ties with once you finish your bracelet.

2. Separate one string from the bundle and make a forward knot with it onto the entire bundle of strings at the same time.

3. Continue making forward knots with this string onto the other strings. You will notice that the knots will start to coil around the bundle. This is what gives the Chinese staircase its name, as it resembles a staircase.

4. When you want to switch to a different color, simply place your string down to join the bundle and bring out the string you want to switch to and make a forward knot with that string onto the entire bundle of strings, now including the previous string.

Continue making knots and switching colors until the bracelet reaches the length you want. Once you're done you can create ties for your bracelet. These are explained in chapter 9.

▪ Candy Stripe ▪

The Candy Stripe bracelet is probably the simplest bracelet you could make. It is a normal pattern and it is often the first bracelet many knotters start with, myself included. The reason I don't recommend starting with the Candy Stripe bracelet is that it only uses forward knots (or only backward knots) to create the design. This means that as you are making the bracelet, you are only practicing one type of knot. This could cause issues down the line if you become more comfortable with making one type of knot over the other. However, the candy stripe is still a super fun bracelet to make, so let's dive into it.

1. Start by choosing your colors. The more colors you choose, the wider your bracelet will be and the longer your strings will need to be. For this tutorial I will choose three colors. For simplicity, cut two strings per color, each 2 yards in length. Fold the strings in half and make a beginner's loop, explained in chapter 9.

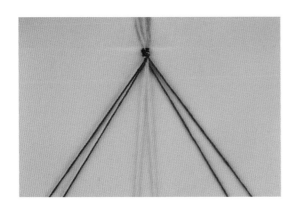

2. Secure your strings to your workspace and arrange them in the order you want them to appear within the bracelet. I want to make two rows per color, so I will double up on my strings. If you would like to do one row per color, you can do that by spreading out the two strings of the same color.

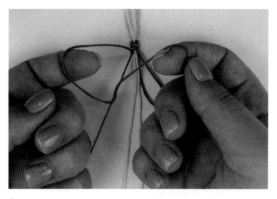 

3. Take the outermost string on the left side and make a row of forward knots along the rest of the strings in order.

And that's it—there is just one type of repeating row to this bracelet. Simply repeat that step over and over until the bracelet reaches the length that you want. Once you're done, you can create ties for your bracelet. These are explained in chapter 9.

Due to the structure of the pattern, candy stripe bracelets tend to curl. Don't worry—it's not just you. If that bothers you, you can try ironing the bracelet, though it shouldn't be a problem if you were to wear the bracelet with a curl.

Half n' Half Chevron

The Half n' Half Chevron is a variation of the Classic Chevron and is thus a normal pattern. This bracelet is a great next step in learning to make normal patterns. It is just as simple as the Classic Chevron because there is only one knot that is different, but at the same time it is visually interesting enough to make it really fun to create and to add some variety to your bracelet making as a newbie knotter.

1. Start by choosing your colors. For this tutorial I will go with four colors: three colors for the left side to alternate and three black for the right side. For simplicity, cut one string per color for the alternating colors and three strings for the black, all 1 yard in length. Make an overhand knot, leaving enough string to make ties with later.

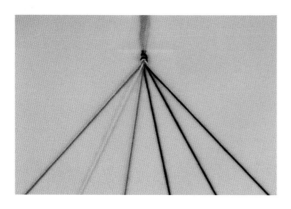

2. Arrange your strings by separating them into two bundles, the alternating colors on the left and the three black strings on the right.

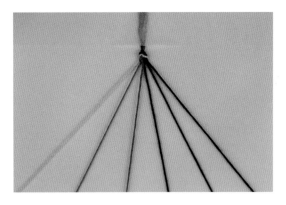

3. Grab the outermost string on the left and make forward knots with it along the rest of the strings in the bundle until it reaches the center, just like in a Classic Chevron.

4. Next grab the outermost string on the right and make backward knots with it along the rest of the strings in the bundle until it reaches the center, just like in a Classic Chevron.

5. Once both strings are in the center, make a forward-backward knot with the string on the left onto the black string. This knot reverses the color string back to the left side of the bracelet, and this one knot is what is responsible for the Half n' Half look.

The first row after a beginner's loop may look a bit wonky as the strings are just spreading out after a knot, but as long as you pay attention to the string order and the knots you are making, it will even out as you go along. Repeat these steps until the bracelet reaches the length you want. Once you're done, you can create ties for your bracelet. These are explained in chapter 9.

Refracted Chevron

The Refracted Chevron is another variation of the Classic Chevron and is thus a normal pattern. This bracelet is slightly more difficult to make than the regular chevron because you need to remember which knot you are on at any given point within the process. However, there is only a slight difference from the classic design, so it is a perfect steppingstone to learning more difficult patterns later.

1. Start by choosing your colors. For this tutorial I will choose five colors. For simplicity, cut one string per color, 2 yards in length. Fold the strings in half and make a beginner's loop, explained in chapter 9.

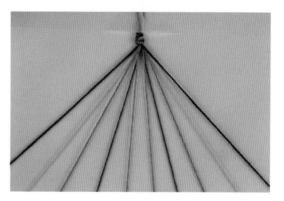

2. Arrange your strings by separating them into two bundles symmetrically, in the order you want them to appear in your bracelet.

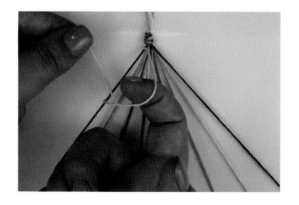

3. Grab the two outermost strings on the left and do a backward knot with the one that is closest to the center onto the one that is on the edge.

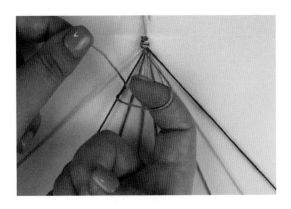

4. These two strings have now switched places. Grab the next string, the one to the right of the first two, and do another backward knot with it onto the string that is now second from the edge.

5. These strings have now also switched places. Now grab the string that we have so far only made knots onto, the green one in my case, and make forward knots onto the remaining strings to the right of it in this bundle until this string reaches the center, just like in a Classic Chevron bracelet.

6. Mirror these steps on the other side. Grab the two outermost strings on the right and make a forward knot with the one that is closest to the center onto the one that is on the edge.

7. These two strings have now switched places. Grab the next string, the one to the left of the first two, and make another forward knot with it onto the string that is now second from the edge.

8. These strings have now also switched places. Now grab the string that we have so far only made knots onto, the green one in my case, and make backward knots onto the remaining strings to the left of it in this bundle until this string reaches the center, just like in a Classic Chevron bracelet.

9. Once the two strings are in the center, make any knot between them, since they are the same color. I will just make a forward knot.

The first row after a beginner's loop may look a bit wonky as the strings are just spreading out after a knot, but as long as you pay attention to the string order and the knots you are making, it will even out as you go along. Repeat these steps until the bracelet reaches the length you want. Once you're done, you can create ties for your bracelet. These are explained in chapter 9.

⊡ Rag Rug ⊡

The term "Rag Rug Bracelet" is used to describe a few different bracelets within the bracelet-making community. There are slightly different ways to make a Rag Rug bracelet. In this tutorial I will show you how to make a striped Rag Rug bracelet with strings that stick out along the sides of the bracelet.

Since the Rag Rug is made by making knots with a leading string in a horizontal row onto unseen base strings, it is technically an alpha bracelet. The beauty of the Rag Rug bracelet is that each row uses a separate piece of string. This means that a very small amount of string is needed per row. This makes the Rag Rug the perfect bracelet in which to use up your scrap strings leftover from other bracelets.

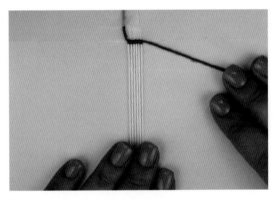

1. Start by choosing how wide you want your bracelet to be. I want mine to be six strings wide. Cut your base strings to each be 1 yard long and then tape them down to your workspace.

2. Decide which color you want for the first row within the bracelet. As mentioned previously, scrap thread is great for this bracelet, so I will just go with a random color I have a scrap of. If you are cutting a new string for this, don't make it any longer than 4 inches. Either tape this leading string down to the left of your bracelet or hold it in place with your finger and then use it to make a row of forward knots along the base strings.

3. Once that is done, grab the next color and do the same thing. Repeat these steps over and over until the bracelet reaches the length that you want. Once you're done you can create ties for your bracelet. These are explained in chapter 9.

4. Next, grab a pair of scissors and carefully trim the excess string to be the same length on both sides. Your bracelet is now complete!

✦ Zipper ✦

The Zipper is a really quick and easy bracelet to make that results in an awesome zipper-like look. The Zipper bracelet falls somewhere between a normal bracelet and a special bracelet. You could technically represent it via a pattern by using three strings to do so, but when the bracelet itself is created you make knots on a bundle of strings rather than just one. Regardless of its classification, the Zipper bracelet is a fun bracelet to make.

1. Start by choosing two colors and a color for some base strings, which won't be seen within the bracelet but will be seen in the ties. You can adjust the number of base strings to make your bracelet wider or narrower. In this tutorial I will use two base strings and two strings for each color, each 1 yard long. Make an overhand knot, leaving enough length to use for the ties later, and then secure your bracelet to your workspace.

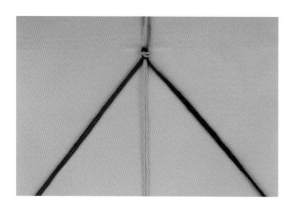

2. Arrange your strings so your base strings are in the center and the color strings are to the left and right of them.

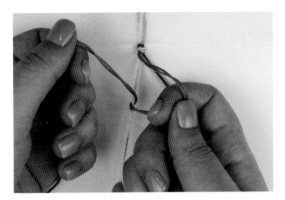 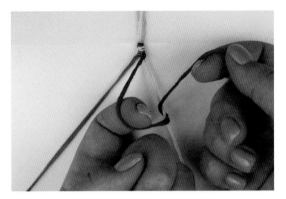

3. Start with both of the color strings on the left and make a forward-backward knot onto both base strings at the same time.

4. Then with both color strings on the right, make a backward-forward knot onto both base strings at the same time.

Repeat these steps over and over until the bracelet reaches the length you want. Once you're done, you can create ties for your bracelet. These are explained in chapter 9.

Flip Flop

The Flip Flop bracelet is one of my favorite beginner bracelets. It has such a cool look and texture to it, and it uses only forward knots. Since this bracelet is difficult to represent via a pattern, it falls into the category of special bracelets.

1. Start by choosing your colors. The more colors you choose, the wider the bracelet will be and the longer you will need to cut your strings. I will use six colors in this tutorial. Cut one string per color and cut them to be 1 yard long. Make an overhand knot, leaving enough strings to make ties out of later, and secure your bracelet to your workspace.

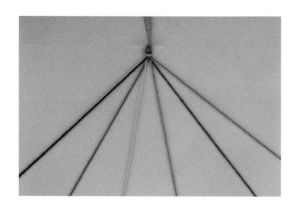

2. Arrange your strings on your workspace in the order you would like them to appear within the bracelet.

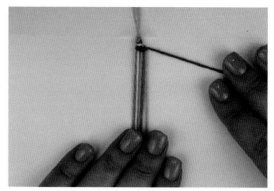

3. Start by using the string on the left edge and use it to make a row of forward knots along all of the other strings.

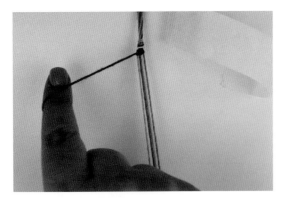

4. Once you have finished the row, flip the bracelet over. To do this I need to first remove my tape.

5. Once the bracelet is flipped, the string you just made a row with should once again be on the left edge of your bracelet. Make another row of forward knots with this string onto the other strings.

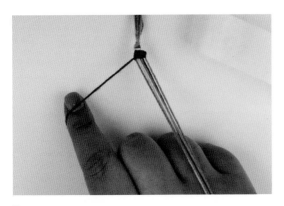

6. Once the second row is finished, flip your bracelet once again.

7. Your string should be on the left edge again. Make one last (third) row of forward knots with this string onto the other strings.

At this point you are done with making knots with this string. Do not flip your bracelet at this stage. Simply repeat these steps for the next color and then the next color after that until your bracelet reaches the length you want. Once you're done, you can create ties for your bracelet. These are explained in chapter 9.

❖ Heart ❖

The Heart bracelet is a classic normal friendship bracelet pattern and is rather simple to make once you've had some experience making easier bracelets like the chevron.

1. Start by choosing a color for the heart color and a color for the background. For simplicity, cut two strings per color, each 2 yards in length. Fold the strings in half and make a beginner's loop, explained in chapter 9.

2. Secure your strings to your workspace and arrange them symmetrically with two strings of the background color at the edge on either side and all four strings of the heart color in the middle.

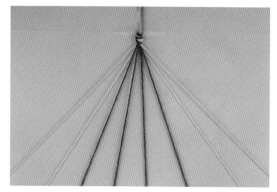

3. Start by making a Classic Chevron row with the two outermost strings. Make forward knots on the left side, backward knots on the right, and once they reach the center make any knot in between the two strings.

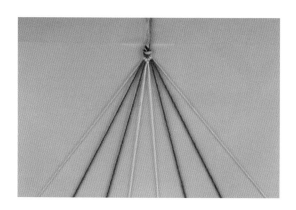

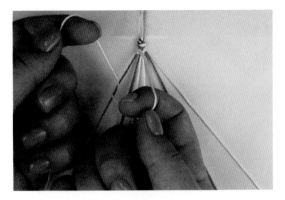

4. Next, grab the outermost string on the left and make a forward-backward knot onto the next string to the right of it.

5. Do the reverse on the right side. Grab the outermost string on the right and make a backward-forward knot onto the next string to the left of it.

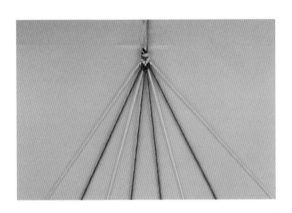

6. Next, do a mini chevron with the two strings we just made knots onto. With the second string from the edge on the left, make forward knots along the rest of the strings on the left side until it reaches the center, and then with the second string from the edge on the right make backward knots along the rest of the strings on the right side until it reaches the center. When the strings meet in the center, make a knot between them.

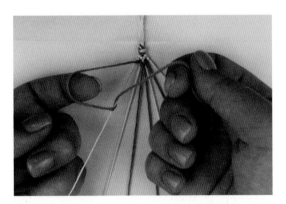

7. Finally, for the last row grab the second string from the edge on the left and make a backward-forward knot onto the string on the edge, followed by forward knots along the rest of the strings on the left side.

 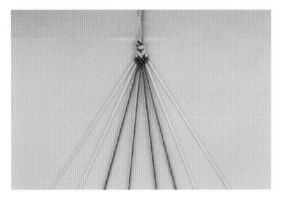

8. Do the reverse on the right side by grabbing the second string from the edge on the right and making a forward-backward knot onto the string on the edge, followed by backward knots along the rest of the strings on the right side. Once that is done, make a knot between the two strings in the center.

Repeat these steps over and over until the bracelet reaches the length you want. Once you're done, you can create ties for your bracelet. These are explained in chapter 9.

Chain Link Candy Stripe

The Chain Link Candy Stripe is a variation of the regular Candy Stripe bracelet. It falls under the category of normal bracelets since it can be easily represented via a pattern. This bracelet is one of my absolute favorites as I love the way that it looks.

1. Start by choosing your colors. I chose the six colors of the rainbow. Cut two strings per color (or one, if you want a thinner stripe), each 1 yard in length. I think the best way to start this bracelet is via a straight start, simply by taping strings down to a workspace, leaving enough strings for ties. Secure the strings onto your workspace and arrange them in the order you would like them to appear within your bracelet.

2. Start by making a regular Candy Stripe and continue to do so until you go through all of your colors. Next we will make the chains that sit between the woven parts of the bracelet. Grab the first two strings on the left, which should both be of the same color, and make a forward knot.

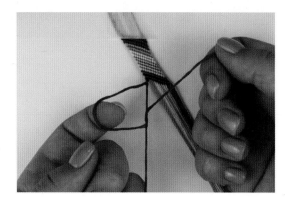

3. Once that is done, make another forward knot between those same strings.

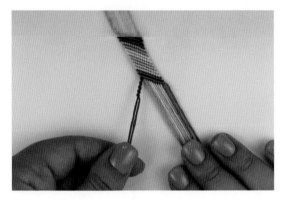

4. Then make three more forward knots after that so there are five in total.

5. Grab the next pair of strings, which should also be the same color, and repeat the process, making five forward knots in a chain.

6. Do the same thing for all of the string pairs.

Once this is done, you can resume making your Candy Stripe as normal. You can make more or fewer knots for the chain itself to either elongate or shorten the chains; just be sure to make the same number of knots for each chain. Repeat these steps over and over until the bracelet reaches the length you want. Once you're done, you can create ties for your bracelet. These are explained in chapter 9.

Distorted Chevron

The Distorted Chevron bracelet is a very simple bracelet to make. It is a variation of the Classic Chevron with only four knots, two on either side, that differ from its classic counterpart. The reason this bracelet is introduced so late in this chapter is because of the start. It would be rather difficult to create this bracelet with a beginner's loop as there are simply too many strings for that. The best way to start this bracelet is with a teardrop loop, which is a more difficult start. It is explained in chapter 9.

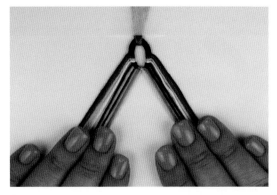

1. Start by choosing your colors. I recommend choosing two gradients for this bracelet, four strings per gradient, eight strings in total. For simplicity, cut your strings to be 2 yards long, one string per color. Make a teardrop loop, explained in detail on pages 108–109, and arrange your strings symmetrically in the order you would like to see them appear within your bracelet. For me that would be the strings of the first gradient from darkest to lightest followed by the strings for the second gradient from darkest to lightest.

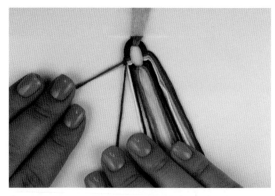

2. Once that is done, grab the outermost string on the left and make two forward knots, beginning the chevron shape.

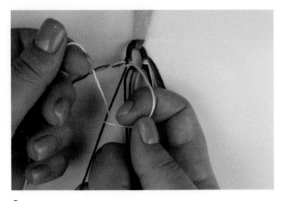

3. For the third knot, make a backward knot onto this string instead.

4. Then continue with the chevron, making three forward knots with the original string.

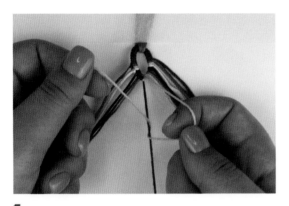

5. After that, make another backward knot, which will bring your original string into the center.

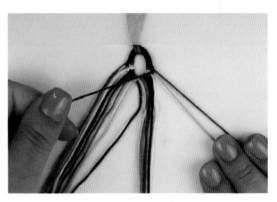

6. Mirror these steps on the right side. Starting with the outermost string make two backward knots, starting a chevron shape.

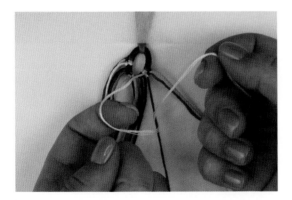

7. For the third knot, make a forward knot onto this string instead.

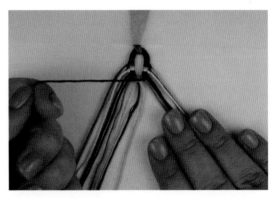

8. Then continue with the chevron, making three backward knots with the original string.

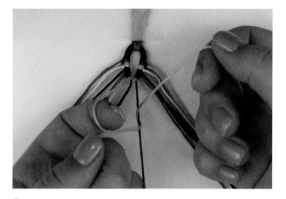

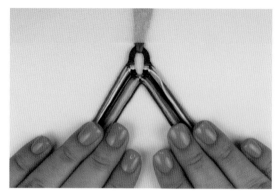

9. After that, make another forward knot, which will bring your original string into the center.

10. Once that is done, make a forward knot between the two strings in the center.

Repeat these steps over and over until the bracelet reaches the length you want. Once you're done, you can finish the bracelet however you like and create ties for your bracelet. I made triangle ends. Chapter 9 explains this technique, as well as the technique for the ties.

Daisy Chain

The Daisy Chain bracelet is probably the most difficult bracelet found in this chapter. While it is still relatively simple to make, I wouldn't recommend trying this bracelet until you have made at least a few of the others already explained in this chapter. The Daisy Chain bracelet falls into the category of special bracelets, and it is absolutely beautiful. I love this design so much that I have made an entire collection of Daisy Chain bracelets and I am really excited to teach you how to make them.

1. Start by choosing your colors—two colors for the daisy itself and one color for the background. Cut one string per color. For simplicity, make the background string 3 yards in length and the others 2 yards in length. Make a basic loop, explained starting on page 96, using 13 knots of the background color. I chose 13 knots because I will be making six knots on each side of the bubble. Thirteen is six times two plus one extra knot for the tip of the loop, to connect the two sides of six. If you are making more or fewer knots for your bubble in the bracelet, multiply the number of knots you plan to make by two and add one to get the number of knots you will need for the initial loop.

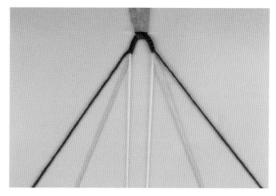

2. Arrange your strings symmetrically with the background strings on the edges followed by the strings for the middle of the daisy (yellow in my case), and then the strings for the daisy itself (white in my case) in the middle.

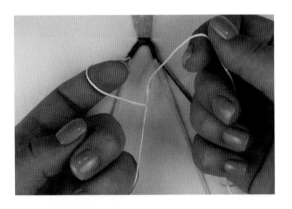

3. Start by making a knot between the two white strings. Make this knot carefully as this knot connects the two halves of the loop. It may be a bit challenging at first.

4. Next, with the white string on the left, make a backward knot onto the yellow string followed by a backward-forward knot onto the background string. With the white string on the right, make a forward knot onto the yellow string followed by a forward-backward knot onto the background string.

5. Once this is done, make a knot between the two yellow strings.

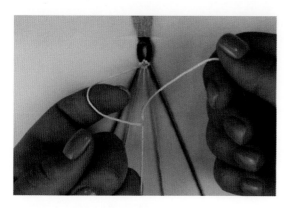

6. Next, make a mini chevron with the white string: Make a forward knot with the left white string onto the yellow string, then a backward knot with the right white string onto the yellow string, and then a knot between the two white strings in the center.

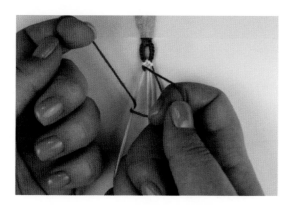

7. Now it's time to make the bubbles. The number of knots you make for the bubble is going to determine how big it is. I will make six knots since this is what works best for me with my knotting tension and strings. You can make more or fewer knots if you wish, as explained above.

Starting on the left, make forward-backward knots with your background string onto both strings of the flower at the same time. I am making six knots.

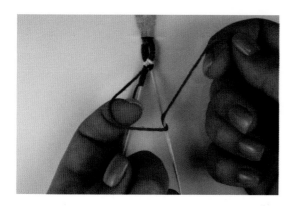

8. Repeat that on the right side with backward-forward knots. Be sure to make the same number of knots on this side as you did on the left side.

9. Once that is done, you can start making another flower. Repeat these steps over and over until your bracelet reaches the length you want. Personally, I make 11 flowers plus the loop at the top and at the bottom of the bracelet. You can make it longer or shorter if you wish.

You could finish this bracelet on a flower and simply make ties after that, but I like to finish this bracelet with another loop. To finish your bracelet with a loop, you need to finish it after you have created a bubble but haven't yet connected it together with the flower.

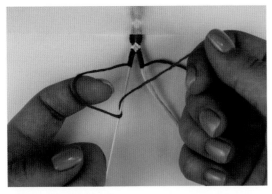

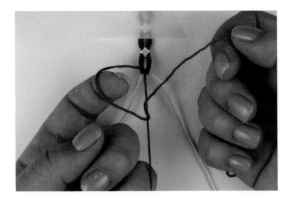

10. Grab the background string on the left and make half a forward knot onto both strings of the flower, just like for the bubble. Do the same on the right side but make half of a backward knot there.

11. Once that is done, connect the two background strings in a forward knot.

Your bracelet is now complete. Now you can create ties for your bracelet. These are explained in chapter 9.

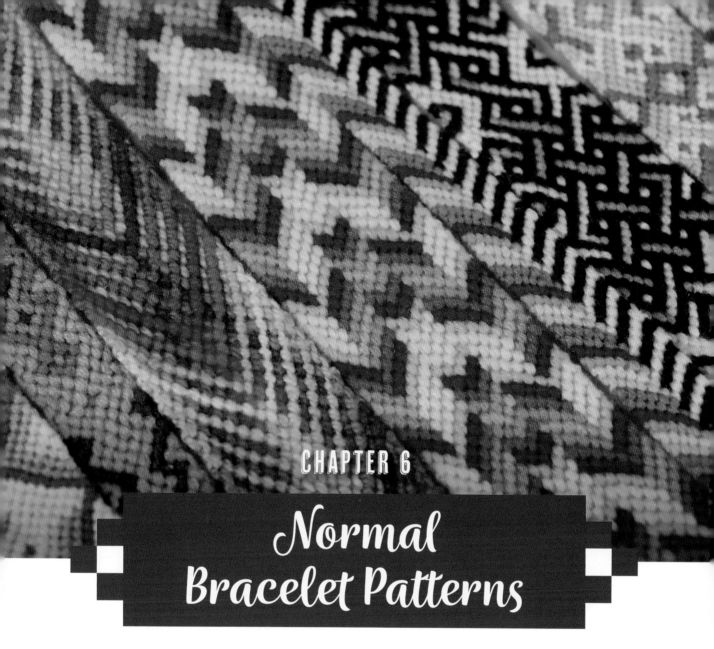

CHAPTER 6

Normal Bracelet Patterns

Normal patterns are one of two main types of patterns in friendship bracelet making. The unique feature of normal patterns is their diagonal knot structure and that the strings within a normal pattern all work together to create the design.

PATTERN ELEMENTS

Looking at a pattern as a beginner can be over-whelming. Let's break down each element of the pattern and analyze its function.

At the top, above the pattern, you can see the pattern preview. This represents what a bracelet would look like if it were to be made using that pattern. Pattern previews are what you see when you are searching for a pattern to create

At the top of the pattern itself you can see lines sticking out from the pattern. These lines represent the strings. The number of strings, their colors (which have letters assigned to them to help differentiate similar colors), and the order in which they appear is used to determine which strings you need to cut and how to set them up to start knotting.

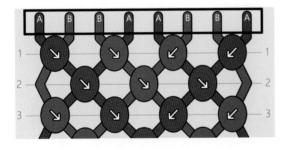

The circles with arrows inside them represent individual knots. The color of the circle represents the color of the knot and the arrow within the circle represents the type of knot. There are four types arrows in total and each corresponds to a type of knot.

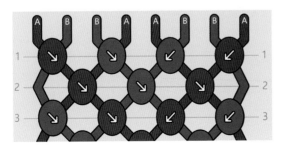

Some patterns intentionally have missing knots within them. These are represented by an absence of a knot in a space where a knot should be. Simply do not make a knot in that space and continue doing the rest of the pattern as normal. Only make knots that are represented within a pattern.

There are also lines at the bottom of the pattern. A bracelet pattern represents only a section of the full bracelet. To create a full bracelet, you would have to repeat the pattern multiple times. The lines at the bottom match up to the lines at the top so once you reach the bottom of your pattern you can continue by following the pattern from the top again.

For most patterns, the colors of the strings at the bottom match the colors of the strings at the top. However, for some patterns the colors change. In such cases it is important to pay attention to the knot types (represented by arrows) rather than knot colors. If the colors of the strings at the bottom of your pattern are in different positions than the colors of the strings at the top, continue repeating the pattern based on the knot types and don't pay attention to the colors. For a beginner, I recommend checking if the pattern you want to make has matching colors at the beginning and end as it is one less thing to think about when you are just starting out.

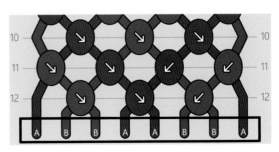

The diagonal lines in between the knots represent strings moving within your bracelet in the process of creating it. Taking note of these while knotting can help you figure out which strings are taking part in which knot, and it also helps give you a clear picture of how your strings move within the bracelet.

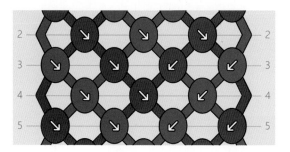

The faint horizontal lines you see represent rows. The numbers on the left and on the right of these lines help keep track of the row numbers, which is useful for reference.

The last pattern element to discuss are the lines that stick out to the left and right of the pattern from every other row. These lines also represent strings, and due to the structure of normal patterns, the leftmost and rightmost strings do not participate in making knots on every other row.

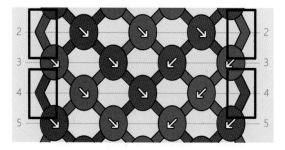

The best way that I can explain why this happens is with the use of a LEGO bricklaying analogy. If you were to lay LEGO bricks directly on top of each other than the wall wouldn't be connected and with a single push it would come apart. Same thing holds true in normal patterns: If all of the strings participated in all of the rows then there would be no connection between pairs of strings, and they would not form a single bracelet and would instead be separate and come apart.

If the bricks on every other row are placed with a slight offset so they sit atop the center of the seam between two bricks from the previous row, a stack of bricks becomes one secure cohesive wall. This is similar with bracelets. If in every other row, the leftmost and rightmost strings do not participate in knot creation and instead the other strings create knots in the spaces between the knots of the previous row, a bracelet is formed. All the strings are now woven together into a single, cohesive bracelet.

READING NORMAL PATTERNS

There are various ways to read normal patterns. Typically, beginners start by learning the row-by-row method to help understand pattern structures and how to actually create a bracelet using them. Reading patterns row by row was the method I used when I first started out making bracelets. However, I now much prefer the segment knotting method. The segment knotting method does exactly what it sounds like: It allows for knotting to be done in sections, instead of by individual knots within a row. Segment knotting allows for quicker, more versatile, and more enjoyable bracelet making. In this section, I will explain how to use both methods using the example of the Chevron bracelet, which was explained in chapter 5.

Row by Row Method

When using the row-by-row method, patterns are created by making individual knots between pairs of string along a single row before moving on to the next row. In the Pattern Elements section found earlier in this chapter, I brought your attention to the numbered horizontal lines going through the pattern. These lines represent the rows, and they will help guide us during the knotting process.

Row 1 is the most common starting point for making a normal pattern, though there is no rule saying that you have to start there. If you would prefer to start your bracelet at a different row, you are free to do so, you simply need to remember which row you are starting with to be able to easily reference it within the pattern.

We will discuss how to calculate the length of your strings in chapter 8, and we will look at the different ways to start and finish your bracelets and how to start your bracelets at a row other than row 1 in chapter 9.

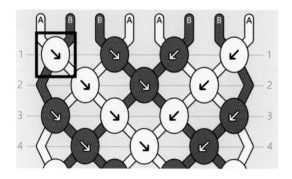

1. In this section, for simplicity, cut your strings to be 1 yard long, start at row 1 by arranging our colors based on the pattern shown, and tape your strings down with masking or painter's tape, leaving a 6-inch tail for the ties you'll create later.

2. The row-by-row method works by reading patterns left to right and row by row. Start by identifying the first knot in the first row.

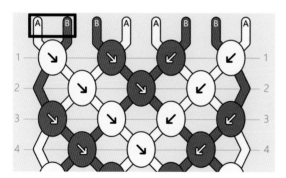

3. Then identify the two strings that make up that knot.

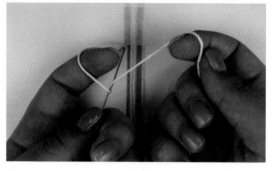

4. Next, find those strings within the strings that you cut and arranged, and make the knot that is represented in the pattern using these two strings.

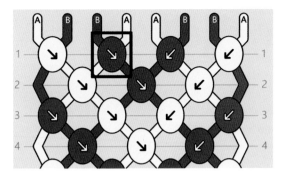

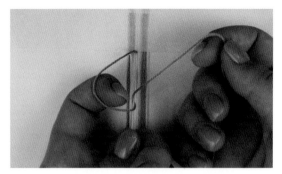

5. Move on to the second knot within the row. Identify the two strings that make up the knot as well as the type of knot being made. Find those strings within the strings you arranged and make the knot that is represented in the pattern.

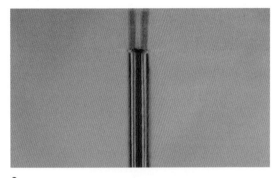

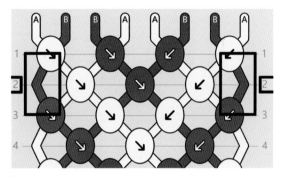

6. Move on to the next knot within the row and repeat the steps until you finish the row.

7. Once the row is finished, move on to the next row in the pattern. The next row will be an evenly numbered row. You can tell this by the number of the row, which is written on the pattern, and by the fact that the two strings on the edges do not participate in this row.

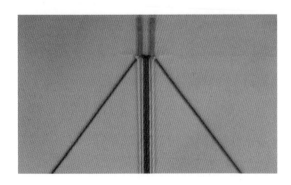

8. Start by putting the two strings that are on outermost edges off to the sides so they don't get in the way while you are making this row.

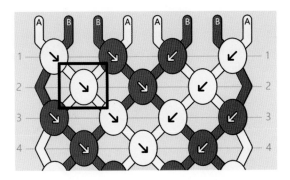

9. Again starting on the left, identify the first knot within this row. Next, identify the strings that make up this knot. These are represented by the lines going into the knot on the pattern. The strings going into this knot should come from two different pairs of strings from the previous row. Identify the type of knot being made.

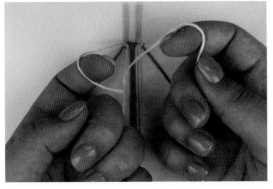

10. Find the needed strings within your bracelet and use them to make the knot that is represented in the pattern.

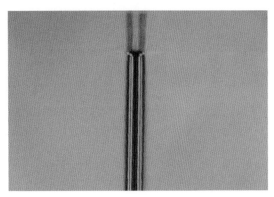

11. Move on to the next knot in this row and repeat these steps, moving on to the next knot after that and repeating the knots again until the row is complete.

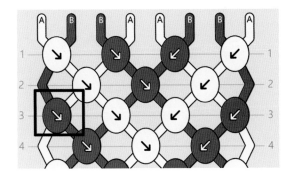

12. Once the second row is complete, bring back the strings from the edges and start making the next row by making the leftmost knot first.

Continue making your pattern in such a way until your bracelet reaches the length you desire, at which point you can finish your bracelet in any way you like.

SEGMENT KNOTTING METHOD

In the previous chapter I explained how to make a Chevron bracelet, which is the pattern that I recommend all beginners to start with. As you were reading about the row-by-row method above, explained with the example of the Chevron pattern, you probably noticed that method of creating the pattern is complex. The row-by-row method has many steps and requires you to change the pairs of strings you are working with between each knot. The way I originally explained how to make the Chevron bracelet in chapter 5 is easier in comparison as there were only two repeating steps: a row of forward knots to the right with one string followed by a row of backward knots to the left with another string. This way of making the bracelet is, in fact, the segment knotting method.

The main principle of segment knotting is making as many knots as possible with one string in one go. This reduces the amount of time spent switching the strings to create knots and, with practice, also reduces the amount of time spent reading the pattern itself.

Let's once again look at the Chevron pattern as an example. The first string in the pattern is used to make a series of forward knots to the right, along the other strings. This is one segment of the pattern and it can be done in one go provided the other strings in the bracelet are in the correct positions.

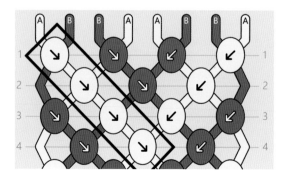

The last string in the pattern does a mirror image of the steps above: a series of backward knots are made to the left, along the other strings, where the string meets the first string, and they are knotted together.

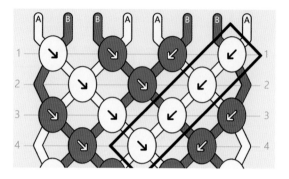

The tricky part with segment knotting is figuring out the order in which to make the segments. Strings in normal patterns work together to create the design and while there is no correct way to segment knot— meaning you can first knot the side on the left, then the right and vice versa—the segments you are planning to knot depend on the other strings within the bracelet being in the correct positions for that. Let's look at the heart pattern for example.

In this pattern we can quickly identify a segment, perfect for knotting in one go: the mini chevron shape starting at row 2.

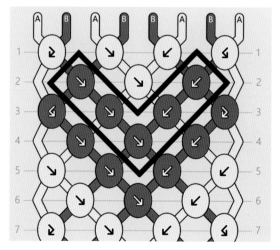

However, since we agreed to start at row 1 in this section, we can't simply start knotting at row 2, so we must first get the other strings into the correct positions. First, we need to arrange our strings according to the pattern and make the knots that appear before the chevron shape. In this case, we need to make a forward-backward knot between the first pair of strings, a mini chevron in the center with the strings of the background color, and a backward-forward knot between the last pair of strings.

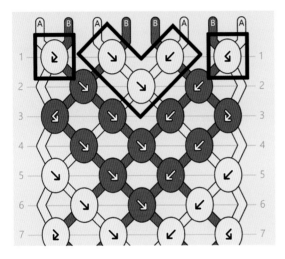

Now that this has been done, the strings are all in the correct positions to create the mini chevron we discussed earlier.

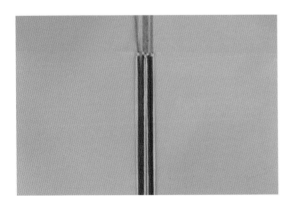

And once that is also knotted, you can start thinking about which other knots within the pattern you can group into segments. The chevron that starts with a reverse knot on either side on row 3 stands out to me.

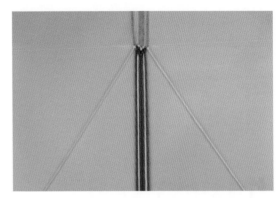

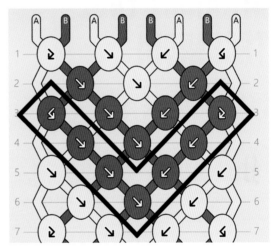

After that is done, continue making the bracelet by finding sections of the pattern you can make in one go and keep knotting until your bracelet reaches the length you want.

This is an example of the thought process that goes into determining how to group knots into sections. Segment knotting can be tricky. A good way to practice recognizing sections and understanding how they are interconnected is by watching video tutorials for bracelets you want to make that include the pattern on the screen and have a visual representation of the section that is currently being explained. All my video tutorials on specific bracelet patterns have this visualization to help you understand the pattern and segment knotting in general. Check out my YouTube channel if you need further guidance.

STRAIGHT EDGE TECHNIQUE

Straight, even edges are often a desired look for friendship bracelets. Some patterns naturally form a straight edge, while others, structurally, make it very difficult even for experienced bracelet makers to keep a straight line. Keeping your knot tension consistent throughout your bracelet and making sure not to leave extra string between knots can help keep your bracelet edges straight, however, bumpy edges is often simply a result of the pattern itself.

The straight edge technique can be a useful tool to help keep bracelet edges straight even with tricky patterns. This technique is not necessary in every pattern and using it is a matter of personal preference. Some knotters prefer not to use it, while others use this technique in nearly every bracelet. I believe it is a useful technique to know and at least try in your bracelets to see if it fits your knotting style. In this section I will teach you the straight edge technique.

The key to this technique is the use of edge strings that are never used to make knots with and are only used to make knots onto. On the left, only backward-forward knots are made onto the left edge string and on the right only forward-backward knots are made onto the right edge string. This ensures that the strings you are making knots with never go past the border of the pattern. By making reverse knots onto the edge strings the string that made the knot always points inward, toward the center of the bracelet once the knot is complete.

Start by looking at your pattern and all the knots along its edges. If all of the knots at the edges of your pattern are made between two strings of the same color—or if there are knots made between strings of different colors, but these knots are only backward-forward knots on the left edge and forward-backward knots on the right edge—you can simply convert all the knots on the left edge into

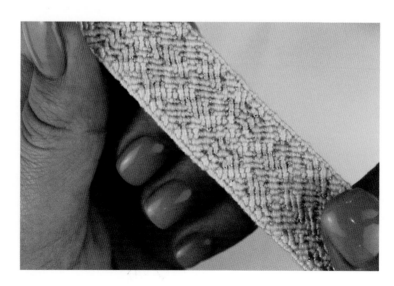

backward-forward knots and all the knots on the right edge into forward-backward knots. This won't change the pattern since when two strings are the same color you can make any knot between them, but it will change the knotting structure, creating a straighter edged bracelet.

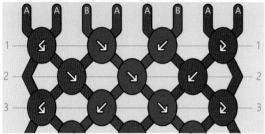

If some or all the knots at the edges of your bracelet are made between strings of different colors and don't already fit the straight edge technique, you will need to add two more strings to your bracelet to act as edge strings.

These two extra strings won't be making any knots and will only act as the stabilizing edge strings onto which knots are made. Because of this you can choose any color for these edge strings, as they won't be visible within the bracelet. However, I recommend using a color that is already used somewhere within your bracelet since these strings will be visible in the ties of your bracelet. Also, if there is a gap between knots on the edge strings you don't want an unusual color to peek through. Cut these strings to be the length of the finished bracelet plus the length of the ties on either end and place one on the left edge and the other on the right edge when arranging the strings for your pattern.

Every evenly numbered row of a pattern will have two unused strings, one at each edge. These will be the strings that make the reverse knots onto the edge strings. I find it helpful to print a screenshot of my pattern (or use a digitally drawing tool) and draw two lines, one at each edge, representing the added edge strings. Then for each unused string on even rows in the original pattern, draw backward-forward knots on the left side and forward-backward knots on the right side.

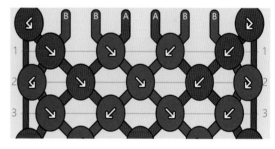

By doing so, you will be making additional knots and your bracelet will become wider by two knots. However, your pattern won't change much visually. The unused strings on every other row are already represented in the pattern preview as the angled strings on the edges. Without this technique, you will never see these strings as actual knots in that spot.

If you don't mind the extra work and knots, the straight edge technique is a great way to help keep your bracelet edges straight.

DESIGNING NORMAL PATTERNS

Designing your own normal pattern is a great way to express your creativity but can also be a bit complicated. There are multiple ways to design normal patterns. In this section I will explain how to do so via a grid.

Normal patterns have a diagonal knot structure so start by drawing two staircase-like lines to represent the borders of your pattern. The row line in this case will be diagonal, therefore, to represent a pattern with an even number of strings, make sure the number of knots per row alternates. To represent a pattern with an odd number of strings, make sure the number of knots per row stays the same.

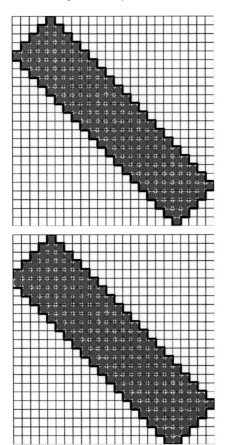

Draw your pattern within the borders and repeat it at least once.

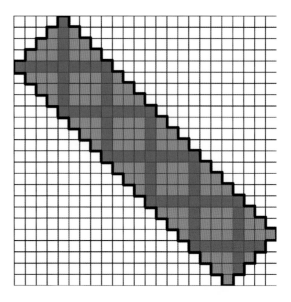

Now draw lines to show where your pattern repeats.

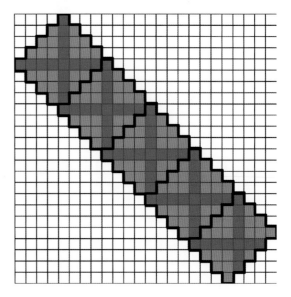

Let's focus on this part of the pattern. Draw an empty pattern with the decided number of strings and rows, leaving the string colors and the knot arrows blank. Color in the knots according to your design.

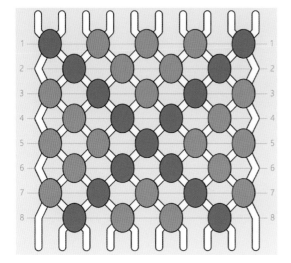

Now for the hardest part: Figure out the paths of your strings and which knots you need to make to create the design. Remind yourself of the four basic knots as well as their representations and functions by rereading chapter 4. If you are making a knot using two strings of the same color, remember this can be any knot as the result will always be the same. If you are making a knot with two strings that don't

need to switch places, perhaps a forward-backward or a backward-forward knot might help. Make sure you line up your strings at the top and bottom of the pattern in such a way that the colors either line up one to one or that even with the colors changing, the pattern will still turn out the way you want. This step is definitely the hardest part of normal pattern creation and its success requires practice and understanding of normal pattern structures.

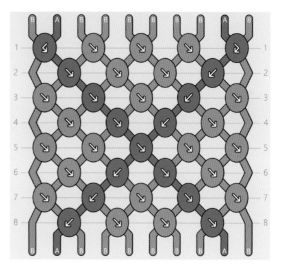

Once you have designed your pattern, you can upload it online to share with fellow knotters. Read more about online communities in chapter 1.

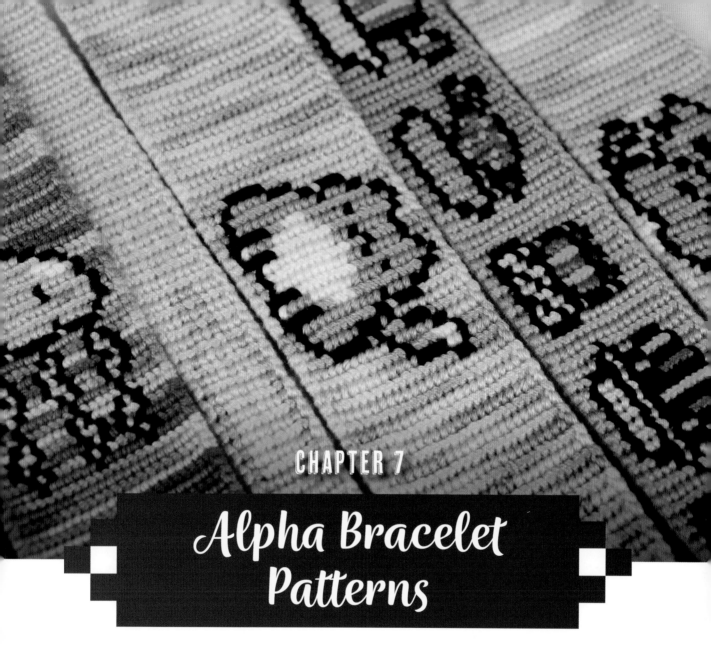

CHAPTER 7

Alpha Bracelet Patterns

Normal and alpha patterns are the two most popular friendship bracelet pattern types. The unique feature of alpha patterns is their horizontal knot structure. Alpha bracelets are created in a motion similar to weaving. Interchangeable leading strings make rows of forward knots made onto unseen base strings followed by rows of backward knots onto those same base strings. Making knots of different colors on different base strings is what creates the design.

PATTERN ELEMENTS

Looking at a pattern can be overwhelming for a beginner. Let's break down each element of the pattern and analyze its function.

Alpha patterns can be represented in multiple ways. The two most common types are via a grid or via a knot structure. Knots in a grid pattern are represented by squares or pixels. In a knot structure, knots are represented by circles with arrows in them that show the direction of movement for that row.

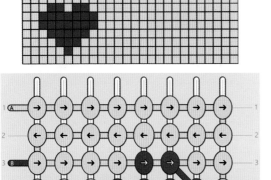

To figure out how many base strings are needed, you can count the number of squares in one row of the grid or the number of knots in one row of the knot structure.

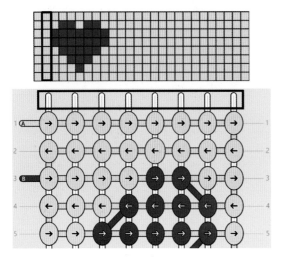

The number of colors you need to create a bracelet corresponds with the number of colors you can see within the pattern. I recommend counting the colors and picking the strings you would like to use for the bracelet before you start making the bracelet itself. The first color that appears in your pattern will be the color of your first leading string.

In a knot structure there are also horizontal lines going through each row with numbers to the left and right of them. These lines represent the rows, and the numbers correspond to the number of the row itself.

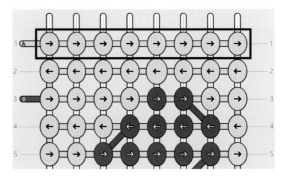

Occasionally, on the left and on the right edge of a knot structure you can see lines sticking out from the pattern with a letter on it. These lines represent strings, and the letter corresponds to a color to help you differentiate between similar colors. The row at which these lines appear tells you during which row this string will first and last be used.

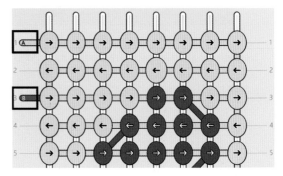

The lines going between the rows of a pattern in a knot structure represent the movement of strings within a bracelet. If you find this confusing, you can simply ignore this element; however, some people find the visualization of the movement of strings helpful to understand how alpha patterns work.

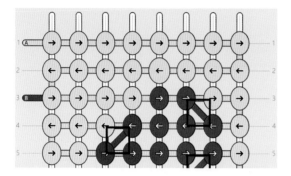

In chapter 8 I will discuss how to calculate string lengths, and in chapter 9 I will demonstrate how to create different types of starts for alpha patterns. For simplicity, all the examples in this chapter will use both base strings and leading strings that are 1 yard long. We will start by taping our strings to a table, starting with our leading string on the left followed by our base strings. Leave about 6 inches on the top to create your ties later.

Reading Alpha Patterns and the Flat Alpha Technique

Reading and understanding alpha patterns is rather simple. Each column represents a base string. The squares or knots on that column represent knots that are tied onto that base string. The tricky part about alpha patterns is the color changes. Since each string can be only one color, multiple strings are required to create knots of different colors.

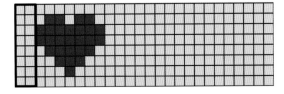

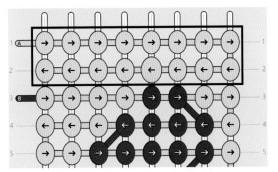

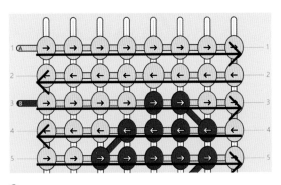

1. Let's first examine the mechanics of creating knots onto base strings with a leading string. In the pattern I am making, the first two rows have only one color: the color of the first leading string.

2. The leading string is to the left of the base strings. This means the direction of the first row will be moving toward the right. Typically, all alpha patterns start with the leading string at the left. This is represented in knot structure patterns since in the first row the knots point to the right. If you want to start in the other direction, you can as it rarely makes a difference.

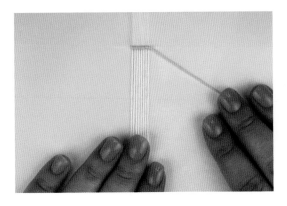

3. Since the first row is directed toward the right, start by making a row of forward knots with the leading string onto all the base strings individually until you reach the end of the row.

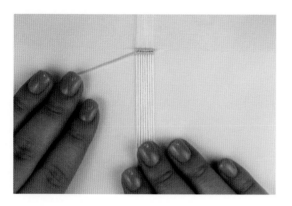

4. The first row is complete. The leading string is now to the right of the base strings. This means the next row will be directed toward the left. Since the next row also consists only of knots of the color of our current leading string, make a row of backward knots with the leading string onto all the base strings individually until you reach the end of the row.

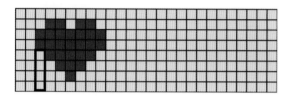

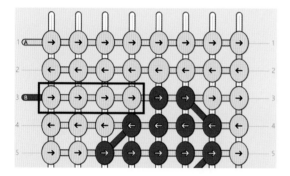

5. Now the leading string is once again to the left of the base strings, meaning the direction of the next row will be toward the right. The row direction changes with every row as the leading string moves along the base strings in a weaving motion.

Continue making these empty rows (i.e., rows without color changes) for as long as your pattern suggests. My pattern has a new color introduced on row 3.

The new color is introduced at the fifth base string from the left. This means you need to make four knots with the current base string before changing leading strings. Make four forward knots.

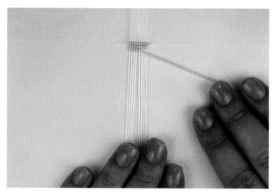

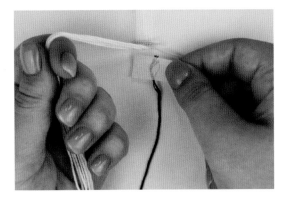

6. Time to add in the new color. For simplicity, cut the new leading string to be 1 yard long. Tape the new leading string behind the bracelet, leaving a small tail of string to cut off later.

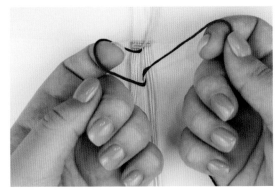

7. Take the new leading string from behind the bracelet and make the first half of a forward knot, or if the color switch is in the other direction on your pattern, make the first half of a backward knot.

8. Take the previous leading string and place it under the new leading string but over the base string that the leading string is in the process of making a knot onto. Drag it across and leave the old leading string pointing sideways.

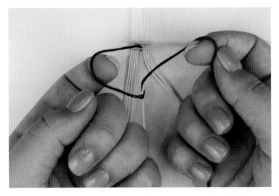

9. Take the new leading string and finish making the knot, ignoring the old leading string.

10. Your new leading string has been successfully knotted into your bracelet. Take the old leading string and place it behind the bracelet, pulling it slightly so it doesn't show up in the bracelet beyond this point.

11. This method of switching strings threads the old leading string through the first knot of the new leading string, tying the bracelet together into one cohesive piece and ensuring that no extra bumps or ridges are created when changing colors within the bracelet.

However, there are some nuances when using this method of switching strings. If the first knot of your new leading string happens to be the last knot of the row it is being introduced in, you cannot switch strings in the way previously described as doing so will result in the tail of your previous leading string sticking out from the side of your bracelet and it will be difficult to hide.

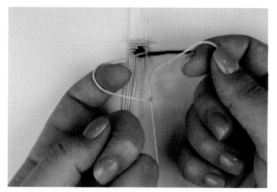

12. Instead, simply tuck the previous leading string behind the bracelet prior to introducing the new leading string and then do a regular knot with the new string onto the last base string.

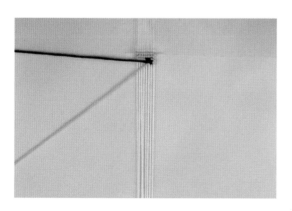

13. This doesn't apply to cases in which the string switch happens on the second knot of the row. While it may look similar due to the position of the knot, it is different because of the knotting direction of the row. Switching leading strings by threading the previous one through the knot of the new one works in this case as the previous string will point inward rather than outward once the knot is complete.

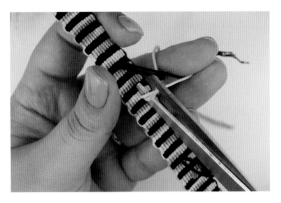 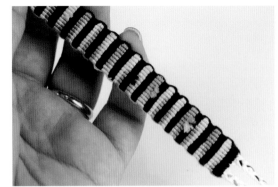

14. The described method of switching leading strings doesn't only apply to switching to different colors. Alpha patterns use up a lot of strings and eventually your string will run out and you will have to replace it with a string of the same color. Switching an old, short, leading string to a new longer one of the same color is the same as switching two strings of different colors.

Once you have created some rows to secure your new strings in place, you can cut off the tails of strings from the back of your bracelet. Some people glue the tails of strings to the back of the bracelet, but I just cut mine down quite short. This is a matter of personal preference.

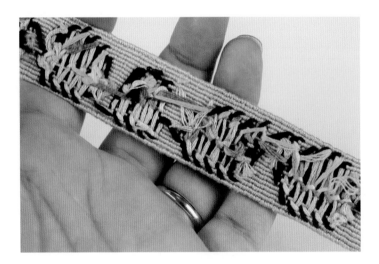

Since backs of alpha bracelets hide the ends of strings and the color switches, the backs don't look as good as the fronts. Some people sew fabric to the backs of their alpha bracelets to hide the strings. This is also a personal preference.

LETTER ALPHAS

Alpha patterns are perfect for creating bracelets with text. Your friend's name, the title of your favorite TV show, or even a beautiful quote—you can make it as a bracelet!

There are plenty of patterns out there that might already have the phrase you want within them. Some of these have decorations or alterations to the letters, making them even more special. However, not every phrase or name has a pattern already made for it. This is where alphabet patterns come in. An alphabet pattern is a type of alpha pattern that has the full alphabet, and sometimes numbers and other symbols, on them. Such patterns can be used to generate any word or phrase, so you can create a bracelet that says whatever you wish.

To understand how to align the letters within a pattern, we must first look into the basics of typography. Letters have various heights. The x-height, which is the height of the letter x, is the distance between the baseline and the median line or the tops of the main body of lowercase letters. The parts of letters that extend above the x-height are called ascenders and the parts that descend below the x-height are called descenders.

To figure out the x-height of a specific alphabet pattern, simply count the number of knots in one column of a lowercase x letter. This will be equivalent to the number of base strings needed to knot an x-height letter.

In order for your text to look centered within your bracelet, the distances from the top and bottom of your x-height to the edges of your bracelet should be the same.

If your word or phrase contains only letters of the x-height, simply take the number of base strings needed for the x-height and add an even number of base strings for the edges. The more strings you add, the more distance there will be between your letters and the edges of the bracelet.

If your word or phrase contains letters with ascenders or descenders, make sure you leave enough room for these. To figure out the height needed for an ascender or descender, count the number of knots in one column starting from the x-height.

Once you have figured out the number of base strings required to make your bracelet, you can start knotting your design by following the pattern for one letter at a time. Make sure to always keep track of where the x-line is relative to your base strings so that your text appears on one line.

STRAIGHT EDGE TECHNIQUE

When making only forward knots or only backward knots within an alpha bracelet, you may notice that the bracelet ends up with bumps along its edges.

To keep the edges of an alpha bracelet straight, make only backward-forward knots on the left edge string of your bracelet and make only forward-backward knots on the right edge string of your bracelet.

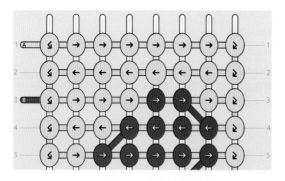

Remember that each reverse knot counts only for one row. So, if you are finishing a row of forward knots with a forward-backward knot, you need to make another forward-backward knot onto that same base string again to start the next row.

The use of the straight edge technique is determined by personal preference, and some knotters prefer the look of their bracelets without it.

DESIGNING ALPHA PATTERNS

Alpha patterns are essentially pixel art. Create an empty grid on your computer and set its dimensions to be the same as the pattern you wish to create. There are websites online to help you do this. Alternatively, you could use a piece of graph paper and simply draw edges to represent the borders of your pattern. Once you have a base, fill in the squares or pixels with the colors you want, creating your design.

Typically, the goal is to create a beautiful design in as few knots as possible so you can comfortably make and wear it as a bracelet. Bigger designs can also be fun and can be made into wall hangings or even used for other crafts such as cross stitch.

Pixel art techniques and skills are transferable to the creation of alpha patterns. However, you must remember that it could be difficult to color match strings to a pattern if there are multiple similar colors within the pattern, so shading could be difficult.

Websites exist that allow you to upload an image and convert it into an alpha pattern. This method is great to achieve a rough outline of what the final pattern might look like, but it requires heavy editing and tweaking to make sure the design doesn't have too many similar colors or random knots.

Some websites also allow you to upload custom fonts to be converted into either alphabet patterns or simple words or phrases. Oftentimes these patterns will require manual tweaking, but they can provide a great starting point.

Regardless of how you create your pattern, online spaces and communities are a great way to share your designs with fellow knotters and to find the designs of others. Read more about online communities in chapter 1.

TIPS & TRICKS

There are some tips about making alpha bracelets that I've picked up over the years. I'd like to share them with you!

■ Use a ruler when making alphas. A ruler is helpful to make sure your rows are horizontal, and if there is some waviness, you can use the ruler to push your knots up or down to even out the row. A ruler is also useful to keep track of your bracelet edges to make sure they are straight. If the edges aren't straight, you can use your fingers to push or pull on the edges to even them out. Finally, a ruler is useful to push your bracelet along a hard surface like a table to make sure it is flat and to help smooth out any bumps on it.

■ Don't overtighten your knots. Tight knots are harder to later manipulate. Pushing and pulling a looser knot is much easier and will make fixing mistakes easier.

■ Use the same size strings. Using strings that produce the same-sized knots is incredibly important, as you want all your knots to be consistent in size. Knots of differing sizes will create waves and bumps along your rows. Using strings of the same brand and size is the best practice in alpha bracelets.

■ Use multiple leading strings for the same color if you need to make knots that are far apart. If you have some knots on the far left and some knots on the far right of a row for the same color, using separate strings for them eliminates having to drag that string across the entire piece, which is what often creates bumps or constricts your work. I often use separate strings for the same color if I have a background color or an outline in my piece.

■ Count how many rows are in a half-inch of your work to help you center a design. Often a design is relatively small, and you need to make empty background knots at the start and end of your bracelet. Make about a half-inch of empty knots and count how many rows you have made. The number of knots you make will depend on the strings you are using and on your knot tension. Decide how long you want your bracelet to be. I typically make mine five-and-a-half inches long. Multiply the length you want your finished bracelet to be by the number of rows you have in a half-inch of your bracelet. This will give you the total number of rows you need to make to achieve that length. Count how many rows your design takes up. You can see this on the pattern itself. Take the total number of rows, subtract the number of rows the design takes up, and then divide that by two. This will give you how many rows you need to make before starting your design. Once you have made those rows, you can make your design, and then you need to once again make this number of empty rows to finish your bracelet.

CHAPTER 8

String Lengths

Estimating string lengths can be tricky. The amount of string you need depends on the type of bracelet you are making, the pattern itself, the kind and brand of strings you are using, how loosely or tightly you make your knots, how long you want the bracelet to be, what kind of start you are making, as well as many other factors.

NORMAL BRACELETS

The length of strings in normal bracelets mostly depends on how much each string will be used within the bracelet, how many knots will be made with it, and how long the finished bracelet is going to be. The longer the bracelet and the more knots a string needs to make within it, the longer that string needs to be.

The average length of a string in a normal bracelet is 1 yard or 2 yards if you start by folding the string to make a loop. If your pattern shows that a string will only be used to make a couple of knots within the bracelet, that string can be shorter. On the other hand, if you can tell a string will be making many knots within the bracelet, that string will need to be longer. The type of start you are making will also determine if your strings need to be longer.

If you run out of string while making the bracelet, more string can be added. I explain how to add more strings in chapter 11. If you finish your bracelet and have strings left over, you can use the excess strings in a future bracelet.

ALPHA BRACELETS

There are two types of strings in alpha bracelets: leading strings, which make the knots, and base strings, onto which knots are made.

BASE STRINGS

The length of your base strings mostly depends on how long the finished bracelet is going to be. Since base strings never make knots of their own, they don't get shorter in the knotting process. Whatever length they are at the beginning of the knotting process will be the length they end up at the end.

Decide how long you want your bracelet to be or calculate the length it will end up being by dividing the number of rows in your pattern by how many rows of your knotting fit into one-half inch, and then measure out that much string for your base string. Add an extra inch as a precaution, and then add some more length for a loop, ties, or whatever start or finish you plan on making for your bracelet.

If you are not making ties but plan to cut the strings off close to the end of your design, for a bookmark for example, still add another 4–6 inches to the length of the base strings so you have something to hold onto and can actually make knots on when you get to the end of your design.

LEADING STRINGS

The length of the leading strings in an alpha bracelet mostly depends on how much that string will be used within the design. If a pattern requires only a few knots to be made with a color, then a short string is required. Because of this, scrap thread (i.e., cuttings left over from previously made bracelets) can often be used when knotting an alpha bracelet.

If the pattern indicates you will need to make a lot of knots of a certain color, it can be tempting to cut off a really long piece of string to avoid having to replace the string in the knotting process. However, working with a very long piece of string can be

challenging. Long strings require a lot of effort to make even a single knot with, as you need to drag the entire length of the string through a small loop. Long strings also tend to become tangled with other strings, and even with themselves.

Some people don't even cut their longer leading strings but simply knot with strings that are wound on bobbins, looping the bobbin through each knot as they go along. Personally, I find knotting with bobbins to be challenging as it slows down each knot I make; therefore, I simply cut my strings to be roughly 1 yard long and replace them when they run out.

It isn't really possible to figure out exactly how much string you will need to create a bracelet. However, with practice and getting to know your own personal knotting style, you will get better at making that estimation. Cutting your strings too long is better than cutting your strings too short, so when in doubt, cut a little longer and save any excess string to be used in a future bracelet.

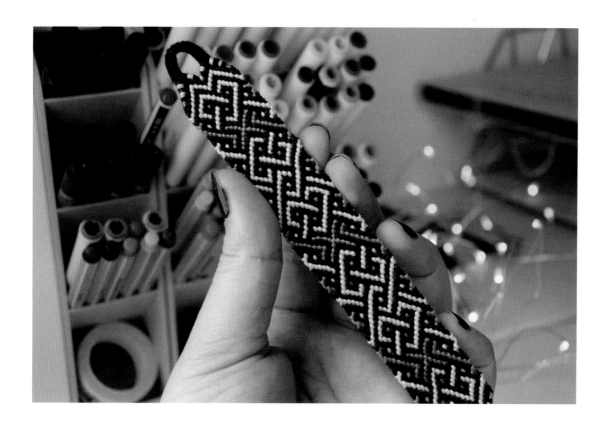

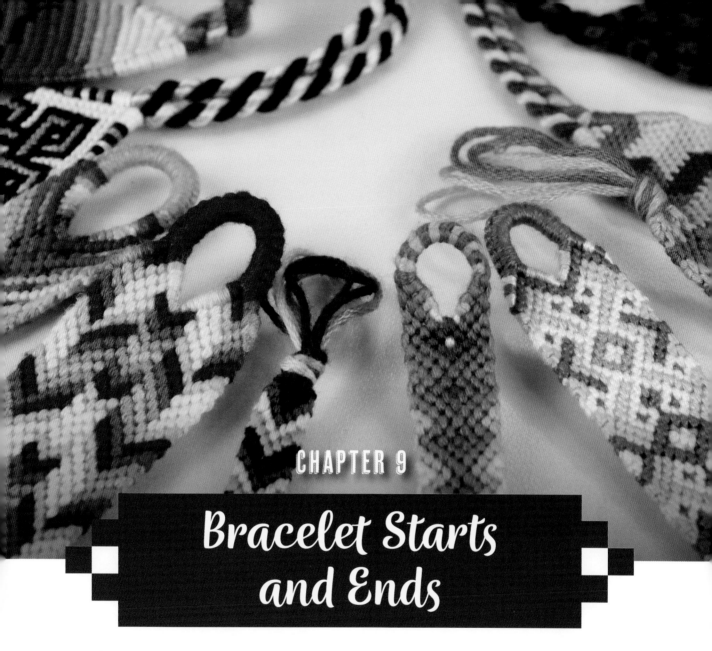

CHAPTER 9

Bracelet Starts and Ends

There are many ways to start and end your friendship bracelets. Different starts and ends have different aesthetics and uses. In this chapter I will walk you through how to create some of the most popular methods to start and end both normal and alpha patterns as well as how to actually use these starts and ends to secure bracelets to a wrist.

LOOPS

Loops are typically my start of choice. I like how a loop looks on a bracelet and I think it creates a beautiful, clean start. Additionally, loops use up less string than a bracelet with ties at either end since you only need ties on one end of the bracelet. There are many types of loops in bracelet making. In this section I will go over the most popular types.

One thing to remember about loops is that in order to make one, you need to fold your strings in half. This process creates two strings for knotting out of one, and it means you need to double the lengths of your strings to account for the fold, after which the strings will become their normal lengths.

This is also the reason some patterns are easier to create loops for than others. The easiest pattern to make a loop for is one that has an even number of strings for each color (since when you fold a string, you create two ends, which is an even number) and one in which the colors are balanced on either side of the bracelet, meaning there is the same number of strings per color on the left and right sides of the pattern relative to its center (since when you fold a string, the ends created are on different sides of the loop). There are ways to create loops for patterns with an odd number of strings per color, and I discuss some of them in the Other Loops section of this chapter. But first, let's talk about the simpler beginner and basic loops.

Beginner Loop

The beginner loop is not the cleanest or prettiest type of loop, but it serves a clear function: It is the easiest loop for beginners to make. And for this reason, it is the first loop I will teach you how to make. A beginner loop is simply just an overhand knot over folded strings.

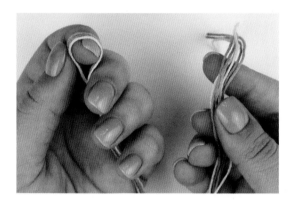

1. Cut the strings required for your pattern. Make sure it is a pattern with an even number of strings per color so that when you fold the strings, you will create an even number of strings. Make sure to also double the length of your strings when cutting them, since folding your strings will also halve their length.

2. Once your strings are cut, grab both ends of your strings, put the ends together, and then run your hand along the strings to find the central point of the fold. This will be the tip of your loop.

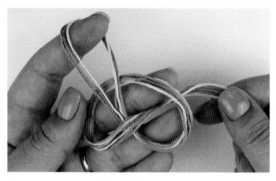

3. Whatever size you make the loop at this stage is the size it will end up being. Loop sizes are personal preference. I prefer a small loop as I think it looks neater, but it must be big enough for at least one tie of your bracelet to fit through. Decide how big your loop will be by choosing the point at which you want your bracelet to start. Hold your fingers at that point to keep track of it, make an overhand knot with your other hand, and then tighten that knot as close as you can to that point, as shown in these figures.

The beginner loop is done! You are ready to secure your bracelet to your workspace and start knotting.

❖ Basic Loops ❖

Basic loops are the foundation of many types of brace-let loops. While I rarely just go for a basic loop as my bracelet start, basic loops are at the core of teardrop loops and triangle ends after loops, which are my favorite types of starts. In this section I'll teach you how to create the basic loops.

SINGLE-COLORED BASIC LOOPS

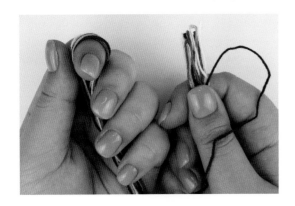

1. To create a single-colored basic loop, you must first choose the color you would like your loop to be. I like to complement the bracelet itself with the colors of my loops, so I tend to go for the color that is most dominant in the pattern or the color of the outline within the design of the bracelet. The color to choose is up to you. Once you have selected your color, you will cut that string roughly 4 inches longer than the rest of your strings to accommodate for the creation of the loop.

Once you have cut your strings, fold them in half, except for the string with the added 4 inches. This string won't be folded in half; instead the extra 4 inches will be on one side.

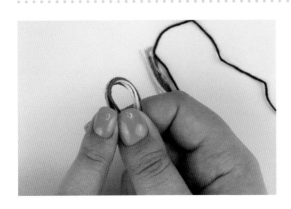

2. Decide how big you want your loop to be and grab the place you want your bracelet to start at with your fingers, marking that spot. Make sure that spot is on the side that is opposite the side of the longer end of the string for the loop's color.

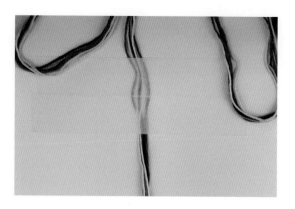

3. Unfold your strings and secure them to your workplace at the spot you marked in the previous step. If you are using tape, tape it down at that spot. Otherwise, make an overhand knot at that spot to help you secure your strings. You will later undo this overhand knot after the loop is complete.

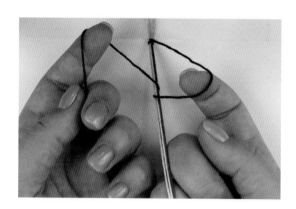

4. Grab the string you chose for the loop's color that has the extra 4 inches and make a forward-backward knot onto the entire bundle of the rest of the strings.

5. Continue making forward-backward knots onto the bundle of strings until your loop reaches the length you desire. I find it helpful to fold the newly formed loop every once in a while to check if it has reached the length I want. There is no set number of knots you need to do as the loop length will differ from pattern to pattern and is based on personal preference. Once you are done, you can undo your strings from your workplace, fold the loop, and start working on your bracelet.

MULTICOLORED BASIC LOOPS

Multicolored basic loops are created the same way as regular basic loops. The only difference is that you select multiple colors and, thus, multiple strings to create the loop itself. Multicolored basic loops can be created with any number of strings and colors, but for simplicity, I will use just two colors in this tutorial.

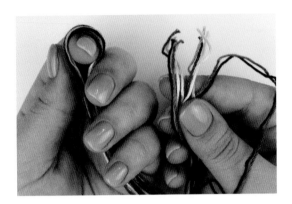

1. Start by selecting the colors you would like for your loop. As I mentioned, I like to use my loops to complement the bracelet itself, so if a bracelet uses alternating colors or a gradient, I might select my colors accordingly to highlight those colors in the loop. Once you have selected your colors, you will need to cut those strings roughly 3 inches longer than the rest to accommodate the creation of the loop. The more colors you choose for your loop, the less additional length you will need for each color.

Once you have cut your strings, fold them in half, except for the strings with the extra length. These strings won't be folded in half; instead, the extra ends will be on one side.

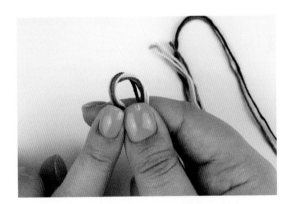

2. Decide how big you want your loop and grab the place where you want your bracelet to start with your fingers, marking that spot. Make sure that spot is on the side that is opposite the side of the longer ends of the strings for the loop's color.

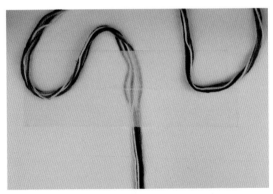

3. Unfold your strings and secure them to your workplace at the spot you marked in the previous step. If you are using tape, tape it down at that spot. Otherwise, make an overhand knot at that spot to help you secure your strings. You will undo this overhand knot after the loop is complete.

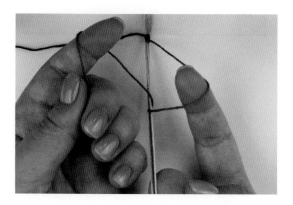

4. Grab the first string you chose for the loop's color that has the extra length and make a forward-backward knot onto the entire bundle of the rest of the strings, just like in a single-color basic loop. Put that string to the side. Grab the second string you chose for the loop's color that has the extra length and make a forward-backward knot on the entire bundle of strings, excluding the other string you are creating the loop with.

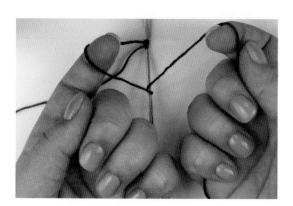

5. Next, grab the first string again and make a forward-backward knot onto the entire bundle, excluding the second string. Make sure the second string is underneath the first string as you are making the knot.

6. Continue making forward-backward knots onto the bundle of strings, alternating the strings you are making the knots with, until your loop reaches the length you desire. Once you are done, you can undo your strings from your workplace, fold the loop, and start working on your bracelet.

OTHER LOOPS

While creating a loop for a pattern that has an even and balanced number of strings is easiest, there are still ways to create loops for patterns that don't fit those criteria. These ways are more tedious, however, and I use them only on the rare occasions when I really want to make a loop for a pattern. Let's discuss these methods.

Linked Loop

The linked loop works for patterns that have an even number of strings per color but those colors aren't balanced, meaning that, for example, all the strings of one color are to one side relative to the center of the pattern. In combination with the removal loop, discussed later in this section, this technique could also be used for patterns that have an odd number of strings.

Before you start making the linked loop, make sure the pattern you are considering making it for is actually an unbalanced pattern and not a balanced pattern in disguise. Some patterns that are balanced will have the first row look unbalanced, with more strings per color on one side than the other. However, if you look more closely at such patterns, you might notice a row in which the pattern becomes balanced, meaning that each string on the left has a matching string of the same color on the right. Since there is no rule that you have to start making a pattern on row one, you could make a basic loop and start making your pattern from the row at which it is balanced.

For example, in the pattern shown at the top of the next column, you can see that all the colored strings are on the left and all the white strings are on the right. However, on row six the pattern becomes balanced with three colored and three white strings on the left and the same on the right. For this pattern you could do a basic loop and start knotting it from row six.

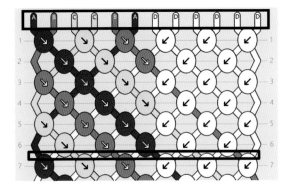

Once you have determined that the pattern you want to make a loop for is in fact unbalanced, or you don't want to start your disguised balanced pattern at a different row, identify the strings that need to be balanced out. Some of the strings within the pattern will already have a string of the same color on the other side of the pattern as a pair to it. Since each of the colors has an even number of strings, choose a pair that needs balancing and match it with a pair from the other side. In this pattern, for example, you could pair the dark pink and light pink strings together and the light yellow and dark yellow strings together.

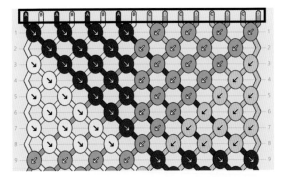

However, if you are doing a shaped start, like triangle ends after a loop or a teardrop loop, which are explained further in this chapter, you must be mindful of where you are starting your bracelet. I want to start this bracelet with a teardrop loop. Notice that I can still pair the light and dark strings of both pink and yellow strings together, as I could have, had I just done a straight start. However, the light and dark pink strings have switched sides. If I were to do the straight start, the dark strings would be on the left and the light strings would be on the right. With a teardrop loop, the dark strings are now on the right and the light strings are now on the left. While the technique for this type of loop is the same, regardless of where in your pattern you decide to start, it is important to keep track of which side you want your colors to appear on before you start making the loop.

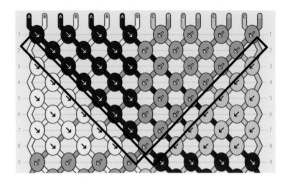

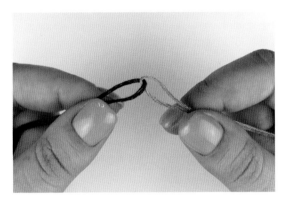

1. Once you have decided on your pairs, fold both strings in half and link them together at the fold, as shown in this picture.

2. Repeat this step for any pair of strings that needs balancing. These linked pairs of strings can now be folded again at the link and can be placed together with the rest of the strings to create a loop. Make sure that when you are folding these new linked pairs you are placing the colors on the correct sides according to your pattern.

3. Once all of your strings are in their correct positions, you can proceed with making your loop as normal. However, if all of your strings are paired, as in my case, you'll have to make half of your loop as normal on one side, flip it, and do the other half of the loop as normal on the other side. This results in a beautiful split-colored loop.

Removal Loop

The removal loop is useful for patterns in which you have an odd number of strings per color. In combination with the pairing loop, these techniques cover almost all possible patterns, meaning you can create a loop for any pattern you want if you are willing to go to these additional lengths.

The idea of the removal loop technique is that for the color you need an odd number of strings for, you fold the string anyway, creating two strings. However, you then hide and/or cut off the extra end, leaving just one end to be used within the bracelet. Make sure the long end is on the correct side of the loop for you to make your bracelet according to your pattern.

I recommend making the extra end that you will cut off rather short as you don't want to waste string. There are also different ways to hide this extra end. The most common way is to simply pull the extra end back while making the first few rows of the bracelet and then cut it off after. Alternatively, you could cut the end but still leave a bit and glue it to the back of your bracelet to keep it secure.

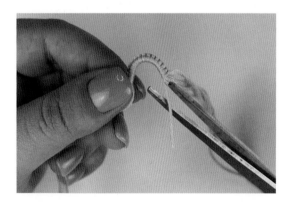

Another way is to wait until the loop has been created and then pull on the long end of the string that you want to keep until the extra end that you want hidden is lost under the loop itself.

Whichever way you choose to hide your extra end, the result leaves you with an odd number of strings per color to start knotting your bracelet.

TRIANGLE ENDS

I love triangle ends (sometimes called shaped starts) on friendship bracelets. The triangle end is my most-used end for finishing my bracelets and, along with the basic loop, is another favorite for beginning my bracelets. In this section I will teach you how to create triangle beginnings and ends as well as how to decide at what spot in the pattern you would like to create them.

Whichever type of triangle ends you decide to make, be sure to always leave enough string coming off of it so that after your triangle end has been created you will have enough string left to create your tie of choice.

TRIANGLE ENDS FOR NORMAL PATTERNS

The structure of normal patterns is perfect for triangle ends since it is diagonal. This type of knot structure makes it easy to draw diagonal lines through the pattern to determine a placement for your triangle end.

Placement

There is never a right or wrong placement for any triangle end in any pattern. Placement is entirely subjective and depends on both the pattern itself and what you are trying to achieve with the shaped end.

I prefer to use my triangle ends to complement the design of the pattern itself. If a pattern has a triangle or diamond shape within it, I will most likely place my triangle end at that point to complement the design.

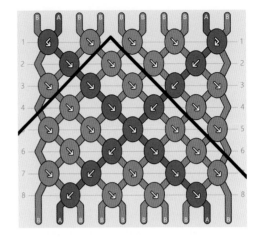

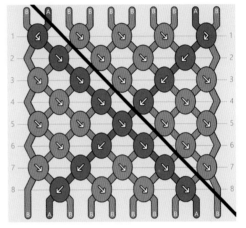

Unfortunately, not all patterns have a clear point for a triangle start. Most people gravitate toward having the point of the triangle end at the center of the pattern. However, there is no rule to say this always has to be the case. You can choose any point in the pattern to be the tip of your triangle end. Your triangle does not have to be symmetrical, and one side can be a little or even significantly longer than the other.

Your triangle end can also be inverted, in the shape of a V. This is how you can create what is known as a teardrop loop. This type of loop is explained later in this chapter. When I make teardrop loops I also try to find points within the pattern that naturally form a V shape so that I can use the shape of the loop to complement the design, but, this is not always possible.

The most common type of teardrop loop will have the tip of the loop at the center of the pattern. However, as with regular triangle ends, there is no rule to say this is a requirement, and your teardrop loop can also have one edge longer than the other. This is a matter of personal preference.

When making two triangle ends after a loop, which is my favorite way to start a bracelet, the shape of the start resembles the letter M. As with other types of triangle ends, I try to use this type of start to complement the design of the pattern, so I look for areas within it that naturally form the M shape. Oftentimes the result is that the edges of the triangle ends are uneven, with the outer edges often longer than the inner edges.

REGULAR TRIANGLE ENDS

Triangle ends look the same at either end of a friendship bracelet. However, during the knotting process, different methods are used to create each end. At the start, all your strings are together, and you need to bring them out one by one to widen the bracelet. At the end, all your strings are spread out and you need to bring them together to a point to finish your bracelet. Let's discuss both techniques.

START

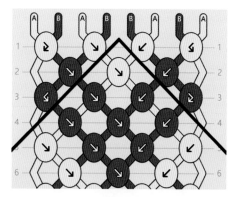

1. Once you have decided on a placement for your triangle end, you can begin its creation. It is useful to take a screenshot of the pattern you are creating and draw a line to represent where you want your shaped start to begin.

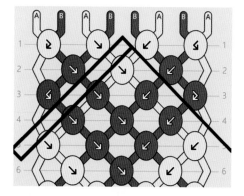

2. Take note of the strings going into your bracelet at the point where you decided to create your triangle end. The strings in a pattern are represented by lines. Identify the tip of your triangle end and separate into two groups the strings going into it based on whether they appear to the left or to the right of the tip.

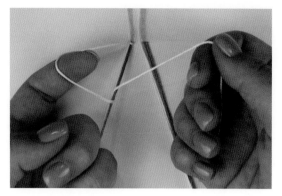

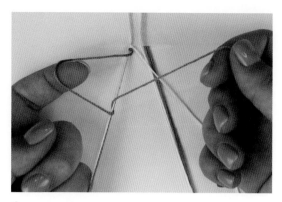

3. Identify the first string going into your pattern that is to the left of the tip. Grab that string from the left bundle and make a forward knot onto the entire bundle of strings that are on the left side.

4. Next, identify the second string going into your pattern that is to the left of the tip. Grab that string from the left bundle and make a forward knot onto the entire bundle of strings on the left side, excluding the string that was just used to make the first knot.

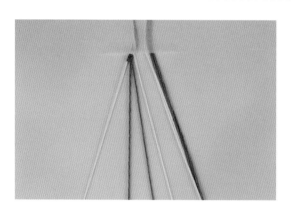

5. Continue doing these steps: identifying the next string needed to be brought out on the left side and doing a forward knot onto the entire bundle of strings, excluding the strings that were already knotted. When this is completed, the left side of your triangle end should look like the example to the left.

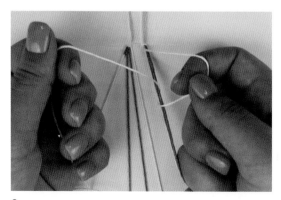

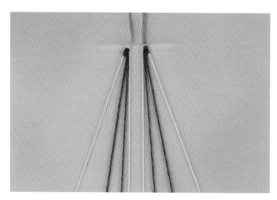

6. The process for the right side is identical to the above but mirrored. Use backward knots instead of forward knots.

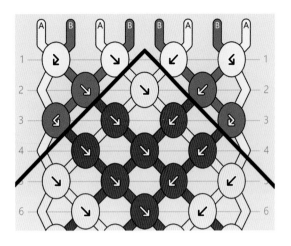

7. Once both sides of the triangle end have been completed, you can start making your pattern. Only make the knots that are within the triangle end and ignore knots that are outside of it. The knots within are in color in my example shown here.

TRIANGLE END

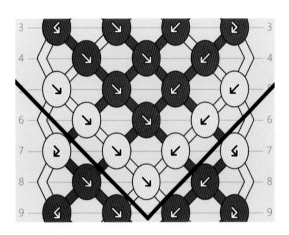

8. Once you have decided on a placement for your triangle end, it is important to take note of the widest point, since that is the row at which you will begin the process of creating the end. Once again, to aid you in the process of its creation, I recommend taking a screenshot of the pattern and drawing a line to represent the triangle end.

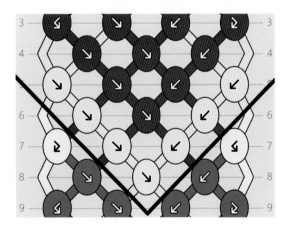

9. During the knotting process of the bracelet itself, you must be mindful of the row at which you will start creating your end. Once you reach that row, it is important to only make the knots that are within the bounds of the triangle end. They are in color in my example shown here.

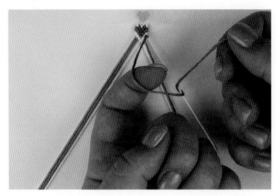

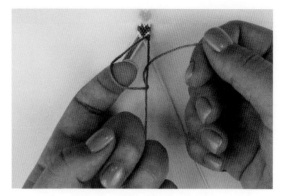

10. Once your pattern has formed the shape of a triangle, you are ready to start bringing your strings together to a point. Start by taking the second-to-last string from the right side and make a forward knot with it onto the last string on the right.

11. Next, grab the third string from the right and make a forward knot onto both strings from the previous step simultaneously.

12. Next, grab the fourth string from the right and make a forward knot onto the entire bundle of strings from the previous steps. Continue doing this until you run out of strings on the right side of the triangle end.

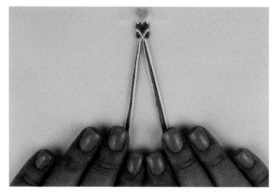

13. The left side is identical, but mirrored, meaning it requires backward knots. Repeat the same steps as on the right side but with backward knots until you run out of strings. Once you run out of strings and all of your strings are grouped together in the center, you are ready to start making your ties.

TEARDROP LOOP

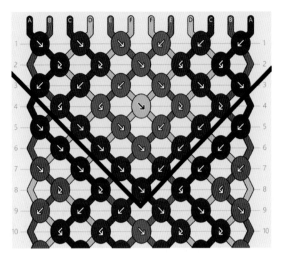

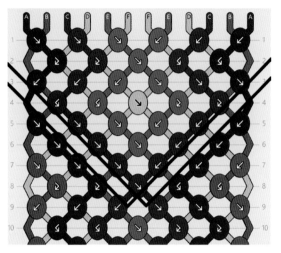

1. The teardrop loop is nearly identical to the regular triangle end except it is inverted. Once you have decided your placement, take a screenshot of your pattern and draw a line to represent its placement to aid visualization.

2. Identify the strings going into your bracelet to the left and to the right of the tip of your teardrop and separate your strings accordingly.

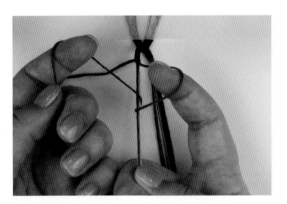

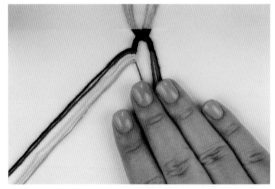

3. On the left side, use backward knots to knot each individual string in the same way you would for a regular triangle end. Knot one string at a time until you run out of strings for the left side of the loop.

4. Repeat the process on the right side of the loop using forward knots.

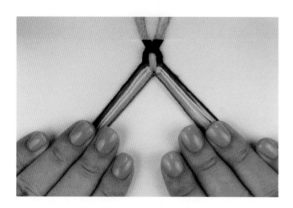

5. Once both sides of the loop have been created, make a forward knot between the two strings in the center of the loop to tie the two ends of the loop together.

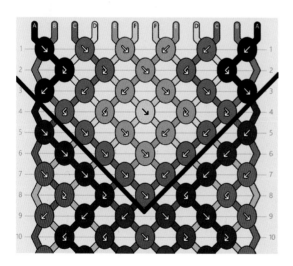

6. Your teardrop loop has been completed and you are ready to start creating the pattern. Only make knots that are below the teardrop shape and ignore knots that are above it on the pattern. In this example, the knots in color represent the knots you should make, and the knots in black and white represent knots you should ignore.

TRIANGLE ENDS AFTER A LOOP

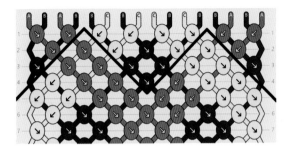

1. Triangle ends after a loop differ from regular triangle ends only because you need to create two ends instead of one for a single bracelet. Once you have selected the placement of your triangle end, the process of creating it is identical to that of a regular triangle end, so you can follow the steps from that section above.

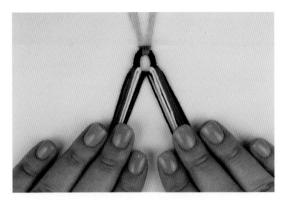

2. However, you have to be mindful of which of the two triangle ends you are creating so as to not accidentally get them confused. Once both triangle ends have been created, you can tie a knot between the two strings in the center to tie both ends together.

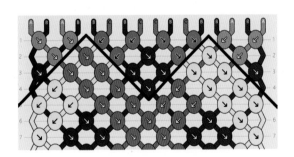

3. At this point you are ready to start creating the pattern. Only make knots that are below the M shape and ignore knots that are above it on the pattern. In this example, the knots in color represent the knots you should make, and the knots in black and white represent the knots you should ignore.

Triangle Ends for Alpha Patterns

There are multiple ways to create triangle ends for alpha patterns. In this section I will explain the most common method, which also happens to be my favorite method.

Placement of a triangle end in alpha patterns is not as important as placement in normal patterns since alpha patterns are highly customizable. There are even ways to start creating a pattern and weaving in new colors during the process of creating the triangle end. However, for simplicity, in this section I will explain how to make a single-color basic triangle end.

REGULAR TRIANGLE ENDS

Triangle ends for alpha patterns look the same on either end of the bracelet. However, as with triangle ends for normal patterns, different techniques are used at the start and at the end of the bracelet. Let's discuss both techniques.

START

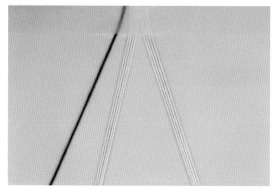
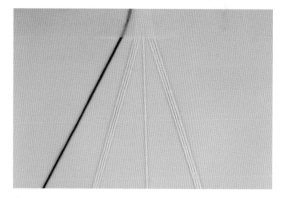

1. Start by determining the width of your pattern. You can do this by counting the number of knots (or pixels) in one row. If the number is even, separate your strings into two equal bundles plus the leading string to the left of them.

2. If the number is odd, separate your strings into two equal bundles plus the leading string to the left of them, and also leave one string in the center between the two bundles.

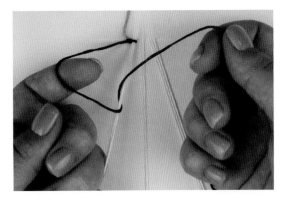

3. Make a backward-forward knot with your leading string onto the left bundle of strings.

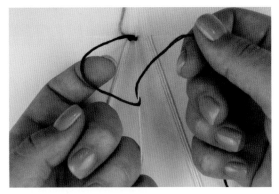

4. If you have a single string between the two bundles, make a forward knot onto it with your leading string. If you do not, move on to the next step.

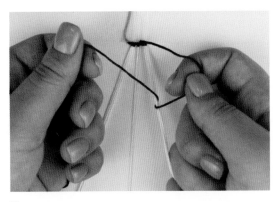

5. Make a forward-backward knot with your leading string onto the right bundle of strings.

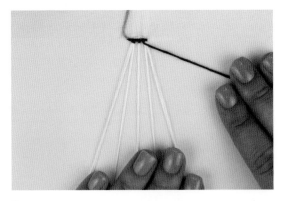

6. The first row is now complete. Next, grab a single string out of both the left and right bundles of string and place these single strings into the center, between the bundles.

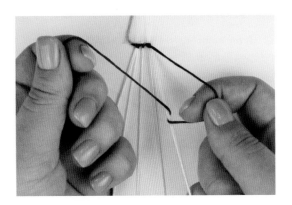

7. With your leading string, make a forward-backward knot onto the remaining strings in the right bundle.

8. Make backward knots onto the individual strings in the center and follow up with a backward-forward knot onto the remaining strings in the left bundle.

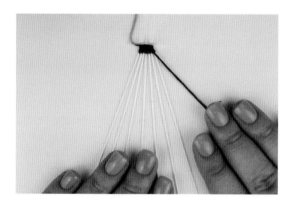

9. Once again, grab a single string out of both the left and right bundles of string and place these single strings into the center, between the bundles. Continue making backward-forward knots onto the remaining strings in the left bundle, individual knots onto the strings in the center, and forward-backward knots onto the remaining strings in the right bundle. After you finish each row, take individual strings out of each bundle, and repeat the steps until you run out of strings to take out and you are making full, regular alpha rows. Once you reach that stage, you are ready to start creating your alpha bracelet.

END

Narrowing down your bracelet and bringing your strings to a point in an alpha is the same as doing a triangle end at the start of the bracelet, but in reverse.

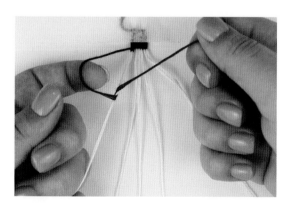

1. Once you decide to start creating your triangle end, begin by grouping the two leftmost strings together on the left and the two rightmost strings together on the right. Provided your leading string is on the left, make a backward-forward knot onto the two strings on the left simultaneously.

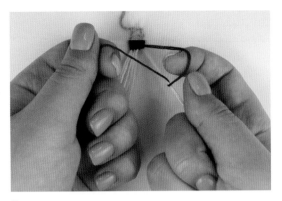
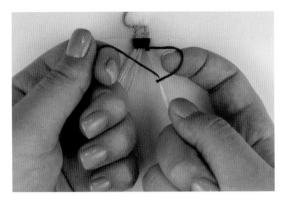

2. Continue the row as normal by doing forward knots on each individual string until you reach the two strings on the right. At that point, make a forward-backward knot on both strings simultaneously.

3. Next, add the closest string to the bundle on the right into that bundle and do a forward-backward knot with the leading string onto the bundle.

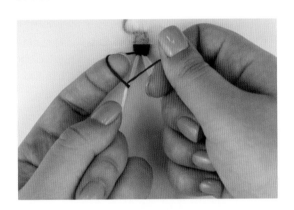

4. Follow this step by doing backward knots onto the individual strings except for the string that is closest to the bundle on the left, which you will add to the bundle and do a backward-forward knot onto with your leading string.

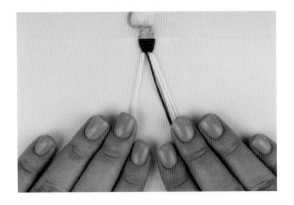

5. Continue repeating these steps; adding one closest string each to the left and right bundles per row and making individual knots on the strings in between until you run out of strings to add to the bundles and your strings are all brought together to a point at the tip of your triangle end. At this point you are ready to create the ties for your bracelet.

TRIANGLE ENDS AFTER A LOOP

Creating triangle ends after a loop in an alpha pattern uses the same technique as creating regular triangle ends for alphas. The difference is that you need to create two triangle ends after a loop and therefore you need two leading strings. The easiest solution to this is to use the string you used to create the loop as a leading string on both the left and the right.

The direction in which you start knotting your triangle end is important since you want one leading string to end up at the edge of the bracelet when you run out of strings. This leading string will be used as the main leading string in your pattern, and the other leading string will end up in the center of the bracelet, making it easier to hide.

To figure out the direction in which you need to start making your triangle end, first separate your strings into two bundles the same way as was described in the regular alpha triangle ends section. Once you have done this, count the strings in a single bundle. If the number is odd, then the direction of your first row will match the direction of your last row. If the number is even, the direction of the last row will be opposite to that of the first row.

Make sure to start both of your triangle ends in such a way that one leading string ends up on the edge and the other ends up in the center.

Create your triangle ends as described in the previous section on both the left and right side of the loop.

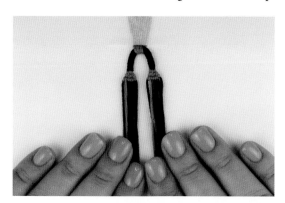

Once you are done, grab the leading string that ended up in the middle and pull it back and off to the side. You can now connect the two triangle ends by taking the leading string that is on the edge and knotting it along all the base strings. If the leading string is on the left, you will make forward knots, and if it is on the right, you will make backward knots. At this point you are ready to start creating your pattern, and after making a few rows, you can either cut the extra leading string off from the back or glue it to the back of the bracelet to keep it secure.

Occasionally when I create triangle ends after a loop, I like to start making the bracelet itself without first connecting the two triangle ends together. Only when the strings within the bracelet reach the center of the pattern and I need to make knots onto the strings that need tying together do I actually tie them together. This means that once I do finally connect the two triangle ends, I can instantly go over that connection with additional knots from other strings to help make that connection stronger and reduce the likelihood of it coming undone.

TIPS & TRICKS

When you are making triangle ends, you are creating knots. Depending on your personal preference, you could choose to leave those knots in your bracelet as part of the design or you could flip the bracelet over once you have created the triangle end to hide those knots at the back of the bracelet. If you choose to hide your knots, remember to flip your bracelet over once again once you finish creating it to make the knots for the triangle end at the bottom.

TIES

Ties are an important aspect of your bracelet both aesthetically and functionally. Ties are what you will use to secure a bracelet on a wrist. It is best to have at least two ties so that you can thread one through a loop and tie it together with the other one, or you could have one tie on each end of your bracelet and tie them together on a wrist.

As with everything else discussed in this chapter, there are many different ways to create ties for your bracelet. In this section I will explain how to make the two types of ties I use most commonly.

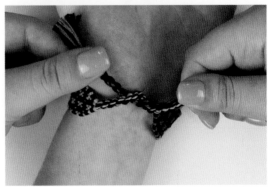

BRAIDED TIES

Braided ties in friendship bracelets use the same techniques as braids for hair, and thus, there are many options to choose from when creating these braids. Let's look at the basic three-strand braid.

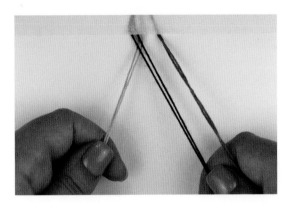

1. Start by separating your strings into three groups. To create a balanced braid, it is best that each group have the same or a similar number of strings. Begin by taking the group of strings on the left and placing it between the two other groups.

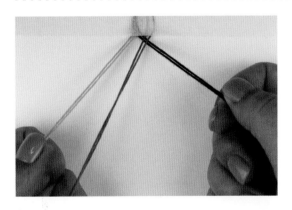

2. Next, grab the group of strings on the right and place it between the two other groups.

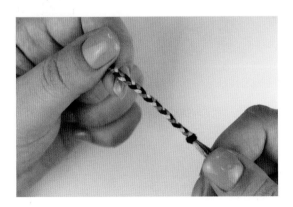

3. Continue alternating grabbing the left or right groups of strings and placing them between the other two groups until the braid reaches the length you desire. Once that length is reached, do an overhand knot at the end of the braid, and cut off the excess strings. Your braid is complete!

TWISTED TIES

When it comes to ending my bracelets, twisted ties are my personal go-to. They are one of the quickest and simplest ties to make and they look great with every pattern.

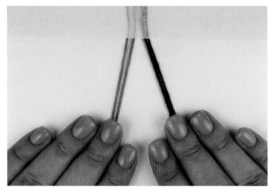

1. Start by separating your strings into two groups. I like to separate my strings by color when I can so I can complement the bracelet itself with the ties. The groups don't have to be even but, of course, that helps if you want to create an even tie.

2. Twist both groups of string as much as you can in the same direction and make sure to keep holding the strings so they don't untwist.

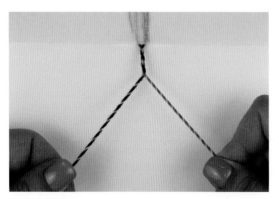

3. After you have twisted both groups of string, start twisting them onto each other in the direction opposite to the direction you twisted them in individually. So, if you twisted the individual ties clockwise, you would twist them onto each other counterclockwise.

4. Once your tie has reached the length you desire, make an overhand knot at the end and cut off the excess string. Your tie is complete!

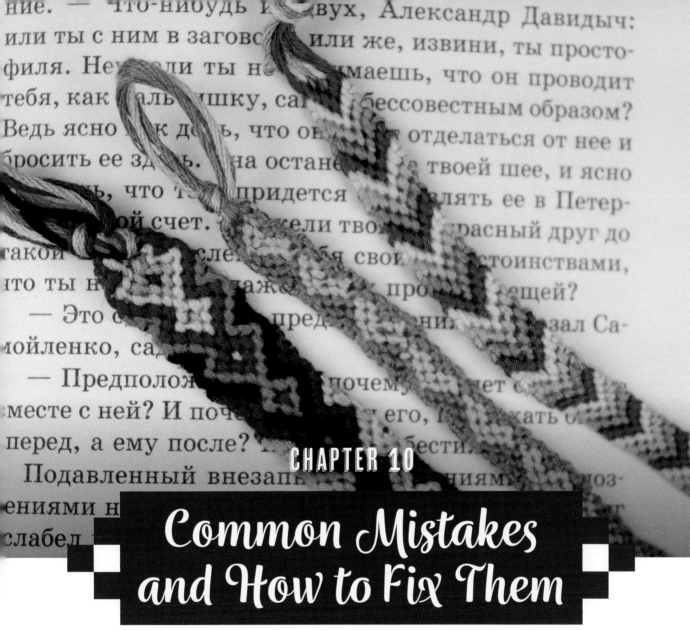

CHAPTER 10

Common Mistakes and How to Fix Them

Making mistakes is a natural part of learning. As a beginner bracelet maker, you are bound to make many mistakes when knotting friendship bracelets. In fact, I still make mistakes while I knot! Every bracelet I have ever created holds its secrets when it comes to all the little things I messed up and had to fix while making it. Let's go over some of the most common mistakes.

RUNNING OUT OF STRING OR REPLACING A BROKEN STRING

Miscalculating how much string you will need to create a bracelet and having a string run out in the process of knotting is an annoying mistake to make. Having a string snap during the knotting process can also be frustrating. However, both are easily fixable by simply inserting a new string into your bracelet.

In an alpha bracelet, replacing a string of the same color uses the same technique as inserting a new string of a different color. This is covered in chapter 7.

With normal patterns, the technique to replace a string is even easier. Cut a new string and secure it behind your bracelet. Place the old string behind the bracelet, move it out of the way, and then simply make a knot with the new string.

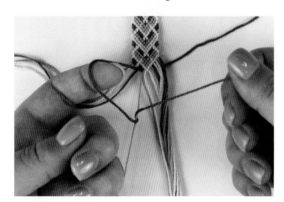

After a few more rows have been made and your new string is secure within the bracelet, you can cut off the ends from the back of your bracelet. Don't worry—it won't come undone.

MAKING AN INCORRECT KNOT

Making an incorrect knot is probably the most common mistake a bracelet maker makes, and it is the mistake I make in every bracelet I create. Fortunately, it is also easy to fix when noticed quickly.

Grab a safety pin and gently insert it in the middle of your knot, separating the two halves of your knot. Carefully pull down on the knot, loosening it as you go.

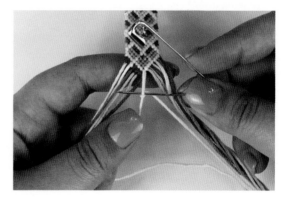

Once you have undone half of your knot, place your safety pin above the knot and repeat the process. You will be left with a curly string and can resume making your bracelet.

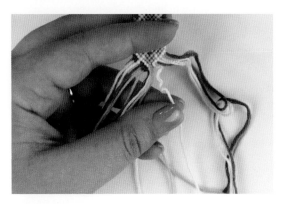

Fortunately, this is also an easy mistake to fix. Simply pull on the string that popped through—maybe hold the knot with your finger to help with the tension—and the string should pop right back out of the knot.

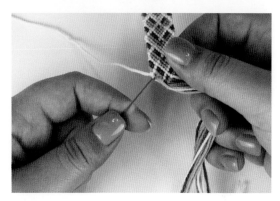

WRONG COLOR POPPING THROUGH

Occasionally when making a bracelet, you might notice that while you are making a knot of one color, the string of a different color (the one you're making a knot onto) is popping through the knot.

ISSUES WITH STRING TENSION

If you see lines of string within your bracelet between knots, or there are large holes between your knots, you need to practice your string tension. The first half of the knot positions the knot. Getting that first half of your knot right and in the correct position will eliminate extra string showing between your knots and will close up any large holes you might have.

If your knots are inconsistent in size, with some being more elongated than others, pay closer attention to the second half of your knot. The second half of the knot secures the knot in place and is responsible for the shape and size of the knot. For the bracelet to look neat and for the design to come out well, consistency in knot shape and size is key.

When tying your knots, grabbing the string closer to the knot itself rather than farther away will help with precision.

FLIPPING A BRACELET

Flipping your bracelet as you are making it can be a common problem for beginner knotters, unless you are making the Flip Flop bracelet, of course. Securing your bracelets with tape or anything that holds the entire bracelet in place, rather than just the beginning of it, can minimize the potential for this mistake. Unfortunately, it can still occur.

As a beginner you may find it hard to tell which side of the bracelet is the front and which is the back as you aren't yet familiar with how bracelets should look. Additionally, in other forms of bracelet making, what we as friendship bracelet makers consider to be the back is actually considered the front, which can further confuse beginners.

In friendship bracelet making, the front of the bracelet has knots that look like small ovals and the back has knots that look like small loops. When making your bracelet, check every once in a while that your knots look consistent and that you haven't accidentally flipped your bracelet.

Of course, there are other mistakes you can make as a bracelet maker. As I am unable to cover all possibilities within this book, I urge you to do some further reading and perhaps find online communities where people can help you with any problems that arise as you create your designs, as I suggested in the introduction.

CHAPTER 11

Embellishments

There are endless ways you can expand on your friendship bracelets. Various techniques, designs, and materials can take your bracelet making to another level.

SHAPED BRACELETS

Shaped bracelets can be made from any pattern using what is essentially the triangle ends technique. Modifying the pattern to create a shaped bracelet can be a fun way to accentuate a part of the design or simply to make a bracelet stand out more.

NORMAL PATTERNS

Choosing the placement of the shaped part of a bracelet is the same as choosing the placement for a regular triangle end. The shape is completely up to you. It can be symmetrical or lopsided, it can complement the natural shape of the pattern, or it can cut through at any place you like. The shape can cut through to the middle, or it could just be at the edges, or perhaps even in the center, creating a hole within the bracelet.

Once you have chosen a placement for your shape, I recommend you draw a line on your pattern to help you keep track. Creating the shape is identical to creating triangle ends. Where your shape widens, bring more strings into the bracelet like in a regular triangle ends start, explained on page 104. Where your shape contracts, remove strings from your bracelet by doing a triangle end, explained on page 106.

ALPHA PATTERNS

Choosing the placement of the shaped part of an alpha bracelet is as simple as choosing the parts of the pattern you wish to leave in and ignoring the rest.

The technique for creating a shaped alpha bracelet is also the same as the technique for creating triangle ends in alpha bracelets. Choose the number of base strings based on the width of the widest part of your bracelet.

Figure out the width of your first row and subtract two. Leave the resulting number of individual base strings for the first row.

After that, count how many more base strings you will later need on the left and on the right sides of the pattern and leave that number of strings on each side in a bundle.

To widen your bracelet, follow the same steps as you would when starting your bracelet with a triangle end, explained on page 104. To make your bracelet narrower, follow the same steps as you would to finish your bracelet with a triangle end, explained on page 106. Make the rest of the pattern as normal.

SWITCHING COLORS IN A NORMAL PATTERN

As bracelet makers, we tend to accept switching colors in an alpha bracelet as a given since that is the main feature of such a bracelet. However, we tend to forget that the same technique can be used in normal bracelets as well. Switching colors within your normal bracelet can help you create really beautiful designs and can add variety to your bracelet making.

The process of switching colors in a normal pattern is identical to the process of replacing a broken or short string, explained on page 120. The only difference is that instead of replacing a string with another string of the same color, you would bring in a string of a different color.

I find switching strings in simple, repetitive, and perhaps even in two-toned patterns to be the most interesting. This technique takes what is otherwise a rather simple pattern and brings it to another level by introducing different colors. I also like to play with color gradients in such patterns, creating an illusion of it being all one color-changing string.

DOUBLING OR HALVING NORMAL PATTERNS

Every once in a while, you will stumble across a pattern that you really love but for one reason or another it doesn't fit the dimensions of the bracelet you are aiming to create. Modifying a pattern to make it wider or narrower can be the solution for this problem in many cases.

DOUBLING A PATTERN

You can double the width of any pattern, but it is easier to do on some patterns than others. The easiest pattern to double is one with an even number of strings and one in which the strings that stick out on every even row are the same color on the left and on the right for each row.

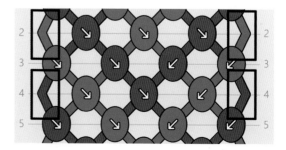

Doubling a pattern like this only requires you to literally copy and paste the pattern side by side and fill in the strings that stick out in the middle with any knot between them, since they are the same color.

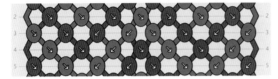

If the pattern has an even number of strings but the strings sticking out on even rows aren't the same color on one or multiple rows, the technique is still similar. Double the pattern by copying and pasting it side by side and then fill in the strings that stick out in the middle with knots between them. However, this time those center knots must be reverse knots. Choose on a case-by-case basis whether you want that to be a forward-backward or backward-forward knot, depending on which color you would like to show up in the bracelet.

If you copy and paste your pattern and put the two copies side by side, and you notice that it doesn't quite line up based on the design itself, you can always shift one of the copies up or down to align in better.

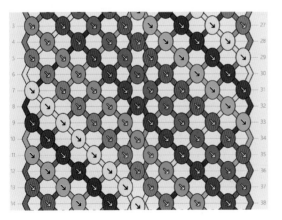

You could even flip the pattern upside down and try aligning it that way to create a new design.

If your pattern has an odd number of strings, you will need to add an extra string for the doubling technique work, making the total number of strings an even number. Copy and paste your pattern, line the patterns up in the way you want, and then place an extra string between the two copies. Make forward-backward knots with the strings that stick out of the left copy onto this extra string and make backward-forward knots with the strings that stick out of the right copy. This is very similar to the straight edge technique, explained on page 86.

HALVING A PATTERN

Halving a pattern only really works when the original pattern is symmetrical. If that is the case, then all the knots in the central column of the pattern should be made between strings of the same color. Simply imagine or draw a line going right through the center of the pattern.

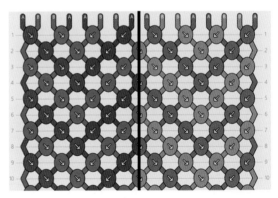

Discard the right side of the pattern and focus solely on the left side. Ignore the half knots that are left on the right side of the pattern and imagine them simply as strings sticking out of the sides, like on the left. Make your bracelet according to this new pattern.

CHARMS

Enhancing your bracelets with the use of charms can be really beautiful. There are so many different types of charms out there that fit any theme or style. Some charms can even be woven within the bracelet itself, creating a unique look for your bracelet.

If the charm you want to use has a loop on it, simply thread your string through the loop and continue making the bracelet as normal. Use a needle threader if you are having trouble.

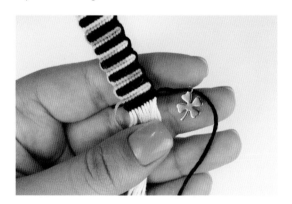

If your charm has edges to which you can attach strings, use a lark's head knot (explained on page 27) to attach strings to it on either side and make half the pattern on one side and the other half on the other side.

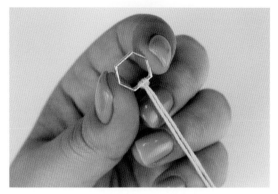

There are other ways to attach charms and even beads, which you can learn more about from other resources.

OTHER EMBELLISHMENTS

There are, of course, many other embellishments you can add to your friendship bracelets. Using bracelets to make watch bands or collars for pets, embroidering an additional layer of a design onto a bracelet, and making frilly edges are all ways to add variety to your bracelets. Once you become more comfortable with knotting, I urge you to experiment with your bracelets. Perhaps you'll be the one to create the next hit bracelet technique that every bracelet maker will be inspired to try!

CHAPTER 12

Photo Gallery

Looking at other people's creations—their choices of patterns, color combinations, starts, finishes, and embellishments—can be inspiring for your own work. This chapter displays some of my favorite bracelets I have created over the years. I hope to pass on some inspiration to you! To see more of my work or to tag me in photos of your own creations you wish to share with me, please visit my Instagram @masha_knots.

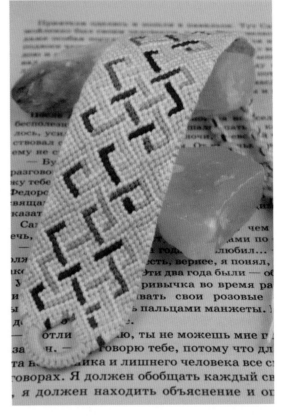

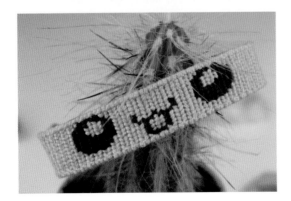

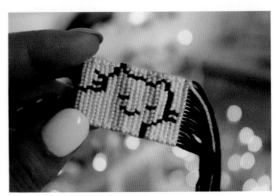

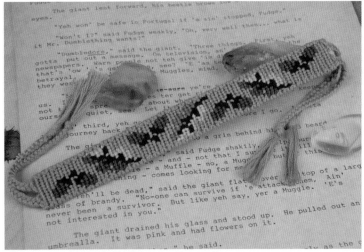

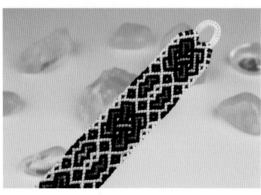

ACKNOWLEDGMENTS

Thank you to Kelly Reed, my editor, who helped me immensely as I stumbled my way through the process of becoming an author, and thank you to the entire team at Rocky Nook who helped this book become what it is today.

Thank you to my parents, who have supported me since day one and who have given me so much. Thank you to my husband, who believed in me even when I didn't believe in myself and who cheered me on through the entire journey of writing this book. Thank you to my sisters and my grandparents, who have always been there for me. Thank you to my friend Tomas, who patiently listened to me worry about every little hiccup I faced while writing. A special thank-you to my cats, who helped me write by lying on my keyboard as I was typing and who kept me company during those long nights by sitting on my shoulders.

And of course, a huge thank-you to my amazing online supporters, my wonderful audience, who have always been kind to me and have consistently cheered me on through all my ventures. I couldn't have done this without you.

Finally, thank you to my readers! I really hope you enjoyed this book and found it helpful. If you make something I explained, please tag me in your social media posts; I would love to see your beautiful creations!

ABOUT THE AUTHOR

Masha Knots is a crafter and online content creator based in London. With over a decade of experience in making friendship bracelets out of embroidery floss, Masha shares her wealth of knowledge in video guides on her YouTube channel, explaining the ins and outs of bracelet making.

Her online tutorials range from simple bracelets explained step by step for beginners to more advanced friendship bracelet techniques and designs for those who are more experienced in the craft.

Masha started her bracelet-making journey in the summer of 2009 when a friend taught her how to make a basic design. She quickly learned more advanced techniques and what was originally a simple summer activity soon turned into a lifelong hobby and a career.

Masha posted her first video tutorial on YouTube in the summer of 2010 when she discovered that very few tutorials were available online and she realized she had the opportunity to help others learn the craft.

From 2010 through 2015 Masha sporadically created video tutorials, but in 2018 she started consistently uploading videos to her YouTube channel. By 2022 Masha had amassed more than 130,000 viewers who share her passion for the craft.

Now Masha is sharing her vast experience in friendship bracelet making in the form of a book to help even more people discover their passion for knotting.

▷▷▷ INDEX ◁◁◁